Martin Dudley was born in
Edward's School. He studied
College, London, and manage
ness School. Ordained in Wal
housing estate parishes before becoming Rector of the Priory Church of St Bartholomew the Great, Smithfield, in the City of London, in 1995. A Fellow of the Society of Antiquaries and of the Royal Historical Society, he is also a Common Councilman of the City of London Corporation, a Governor of the City of London School for Girls, and a Director of the City of London Academy in Southwark.

Virginia Rounding is the acclaimed biographer of Catherine the Great (*Catherine the Great: Love, Sex and Power*, 2006), as well as the author of *Grandes Horizontales* (2003) and a frequent book reviewer for the *Sunday Times*, the *Sunday Telegraph*, the *Guardian*, and the *Independent*. She has also undertaken various roles in the Church, from verging to fund-raising, and is a member of the PCC of St Bartholomew the Great.

Dudley and Rounding's *Churchwardens: A Survival Guide* was published by SPCK in 2003, and *The Parish Survival Guide* in 2004.

SERVING THE PARISH

How to be an effective PCC member

Martin Dudley
and
Virginia Rounding

First published in Great Britain in 2006

Society for Promoting Christian Knowledge
36 Causton Street
London SW1P 4ST

British Library Cataloguing-in-Publication Data
A catalogue record for this book is available from the British Library

ISBN-13: 978-0-281-05718-4
ISBN-10: 0-281-05718-4

1 3 5 7 9 10 8 6 4 2

Typeset by Graphicraft Limited, Hong Kong
Printed in Great Britain by Ashford Colour Press

Contents

Preface

The vicar's wife glanced at the clock, and sighed. Late again. She turned back to her book and had nearly finished her chapter when she heard the slam of the front door. Her husband burst into the living room, flung his pile of PCC papers on the floor and headed straight for the cupboard where they kept the whisky.

'Oh dear – was it that bad?' she asked.

'Worse!' the vicar declared. 'They consistently try to block everything I want to introduce, they talk among themselves and then refuse to contribute to the meeting, and the treasurer tried to ambush me. It would serve them right if I left – except I think some of them would probably like that, so I'm not going anywhere!'

Meanwhile, in the local pub, the churchwarden pulled up a chair to join the circle of dejected PCC members.

'Well, Harry, I told you he wouldn't listen – he never does,' said the treasurer. 'I just have to open my mouth for him to start spouting Canon 21 part c or whatever it is. Our old vicar didn't use to go on the whole time about rules and regulations, did he?'

'And he never lets us have a proper chat about the bazaar,' complained Joe.

'Or about anything,' said Susan. 'What's the point of a PCC meeting if you can't have a good old moan?'

'Well, it is important to try to be business-like,' said the churchwarden, in an attempt to be conciliatory. 'There's a lot of work to be done, and not many people to do it.'

'Yes, I can see that,' replied Susan, 'but just putting people's backs up isn't the way to get anything done, is it?'

In her house a few streets away Miss Tranter threw off her coat and sat down in front of her computer. 'Dear Vicar,' she typed, 'I resign. With immediate effect. I've better things to do with my life than waste any more time on your ineffectual and distressing PCC meetings.'

Contrast that unhappy scenario with the following:

'Hello, darling,' said the vicar's wife, 'you're home in good time. Didn't you have much business to get through?'

'Oh, we got through a lot actually,' replied the vicar, 'and it was really efficient and good-spirited. I felt very supported in what I'm trying to do at St Mildred's, even though we made quite a few changes to that draft policy document I brought along.'

'So you don't need a whisky?' asked his wife.

'No, I think a gin and tonic will do,' said the vicar. 'Would you like one too, dear?'

'I don't know what's been happening with your church meetings recently,' grumbled the landlord of the local pub to the churchwarden. 'You don't get through half as much beer as you used to. Is it Lent or something?'

Back at her house Miss Tranter invited the Johnsons in for coffee. 'You know, I almost enjoyed that meeting,' she said. 'At last I feel we're doing something useful for the church.'

'Yes,' said Mrs Johnson, 'and isn't it good how everyone has something to contribute these days?'

'And did you notice?' said Mr Johnson, 'The Vicar actually listened!'

So how does one get from the negative scenarios to the positive? Is it even possible, or must Parochial Church Councils and all their doings inevitably lead to frustration, anger and disappointment? Our aim in this book is to demonstrate how, with the right knowledge, understanding, vision – and sense of humour – the individual PCC member can contribute to ensuring that PCCs operate, and co-operate, effectively and even enjoyably in the parishes where they are called to serve.

♦ 1 ♦

A brief history of the Parochial Church Council, and its place in the Church of England

The Church of England and its parishes

The structure of the Church of England may be considered in at least two ways. If it is looked at from above, it is divided into two provinces, Canterbury and York, and into 43 dioceses, from Bath and Wells to York, which are subdivided geographically into 8,363 benefices and over 13,000 parishes with 16,222 churches served by 8,897 full-time stipendiary and a very considerable number of retired, part-time and non-stipendiary clergy, readers, and parish workers of many sorts. Looked at from below, the parish is the basic unit, the parishes are grouped into benefices, the benefices into deaneries, the deaneries into archdeaconries, and the archdeaconries into the dioceses that form the two provinces. From above, the archbishops, the Archbishops' Council, the General Synod and the Church Commissioners may appear to be the most significant, or at least the most visible, parts of the Church. From below, the local church, parish and benefice are the most visible and most important.

It may help if we first understand some of the ways in which the Church of England groups parishes and benefices for administrative purposes.

A parish is a geographical area, constituted for ecclesiastical purposes. An ecclesiastical parish may not necessarily be coterminous with a civil parish. A parish is normally served by a parish church, though there may be other churches or worship centres within a parish. A priest – a man or woman ordained by a bishop to the priesthood – can hold only one parish unless permitted to hold two or more in plurality.

A benefice, also known as a living, means the office of rector or vicar of a parish or parishes with cure of souls (that is, the pastoral care of parishioners), but the term is also used as shorthand for the area of a benefice, meaning the parish or parishes that constitute the benefice.

So an individual parish can either stand alone and itself be a benefice, or it can be united with others so that the parishes together form the area of the benefice. A parish has a Parochial Church Council (PCC). Parishes and benefices are very diverse, ranging from the large urban church with daughter churches or church-plants, through the single-church suburban parish and the six-parish rural benefice to the occasional single-church rural parish which has kept both vicar and vicarage, often by joining a group. It is increasingly unlikely that a priest will be dealing with just one PCC.

An incumbent, known as the vicar or rector, holds (at present) the freehold of the parish or benefice (which confers certain rights on him or her). Alternatively the priest of a parish might be a priest-in-charge, who ministers under licence from the bishop.

An incumbent is nominated for the position by the patron; this is known as presentation. The patron of a living might be the diocesan bishop, or it could be the Crown, the local squire, some other landowner, the dean and chapter of the cathedral, the fellows of an Oxford or Cambridge college, the Lord Chancellor, the Dean and Chapter of Westminster, the incumbent of another parish, a City of London livery company, a society created to hold patronage, a body of trustees, or even the PCC itself. The parish's history will usually contain the explanation as to why patronage is exercised by this or that person, body or institution. Once the nomination has been accepted (and parish representatives play a part in selection), the candidate is put into office by collation (if the bishop is patron) or institution, performed by the bishop or his representative, and inducted by the archdeacon or his or her representative. If the right of presentation is suspended, the bishop (perhaps after consultation with the patron) may appoint a priest-in-charge who is licensed by him.

The language becomes slightly more complicated in a team ministry in which one of the clergy is the team rector and the others are team vicars. Neither of these offices is normally freehold but may be described as leasehold (i.e. for a given contractual period, renewable for some further specified period). The team usually has a single PCC with the individual churches having a District Church Council (DCC).

Another type of ministry, less formal and structured than team ministry, is group ministry, in which a number of benefices or parishes are grouped together and may share ministries.

The benefices and parishes in a given geographical area form a deanery. The clergy of the deanery meet together under the chairmanship of the rural dean or, in cities, the area dean. The rural or area dean is normally appointed by the bishop after consultation with the clergy. He or she has no formal hierarchical office as such, but presides over the meetings of the clergy, known as the clergy chapter, and chairs the deanery synod, which includes lay representatives from each parish in the deanery as well as all clergy beneficed in or licensed to any parish in the deanery.

A number of deaneries make up an archdeaconry under an archdeacon, who has certain powers and responsibilities inherent in the archidiaconal office in addition to those conferred or delegated by the bishop. A number of archdeaconries, usually two or three, make up a diocese – or, to look at it the other way round, a diocese, which consists of a number of parishes, is divided into archdeaconries and deaneries. Just to add to the confusion, a diocese may have, in addition to the diocesan bishop (also referred to as the Ordinary, i.e. the one having ordinary jurisdiction in the diocese), assistant bishops known as suffragan bishops, as well as retired bishops serving in the diocese and known as assistant bishops. The suffragan bishops may carry titles of parts of the diocese in which they serve (such as Hertford and Bedford in the diocese of St Albans), though they do not themselves have cathedrals in the places from which they draw their names.

Some dioceses operate a formal division of authority under the diocesan bishop known as an area system, and have area bishops. Oxford diocese has area bishops of Reading, Buckingham and Dorchester; and London has area bishops of Edmonton, Stepney, Willesden and Kensington, and a suffragan bishop of Fulham.

The dioceses in the south form the Province of Canterbury, and those in the north the Province of York. The two provinces make up the Church of England. The Archbishop of York is Primate of England, and the Archbishop of Canterbury is Primate of All England. The archbishops and diocesan bishops, together with some elected area and suffragan bishops, form the Bench of Bishops or House of Bishops. The Archbishops of Canterbury and York, the Bishops of Durham, London and Winchester and 21 senior diocesan bishops have seats in the House of Lords.

In parallel with this is a system of government called a *synodical* system. There are three levels of synodical government: the *deanery synod*, the *diocesan synod* and the *General Synod*. The first consists of all the active clergy of the deanery and lay members elected at the annual meetings in parishes, chaired by the rural or area dean with a lay vice-chairman. The second consists of clergy and laity elected by the members of deanery synods, voting by houses (i.e. as clergy and laity separately). The General Synod consists of the House of Bishops, clergy elected by all the qualified clergy (the House of Clergy) and laity elected by the lay members of deanery synods (the House of Laity). The equivalent in the General Synod of an Act of Parliament is a *Measure* (e.g. the Parochial Church Councils (Powers) Measure 1956). A Measure, having been passed by the Synod, goes to the Ecclesiastical Committee of Parliament and through both Houses of Parliament before receiving the royal assent. Broadly speaking, the General Synod deals with matters of concern to the whole Church, and the diocesan synod with matters concerning the diocese (like the budget and the method of apportioning the Common Fund). The deanery synod deals with the implementation of decisions made higher up and passes parochial concerns – coming from Parochial Church Councils – upwards through the synodical system.

Theology of a parish

A Church of England parish is a geographical area, a district separate from other districts, in which pastoral care is committed to the parish priest – the priest who is said to have the 'cure of souls'. The essential ingredients, therefore, are place and ministry. Parish ministry is ministry to the people in a given place. Generally speaking, the focus of parish ministry is the parish church. There are many variations and exceptions to this pattern, but it remains as a fundamental principle that every person in England lives in an ecclesiastical parish. The Extra-Parochial Ministry Measure 1967 recognized, however, that people make choices about where they want to go to church, and they are not constrained by parish boundaries. It created a sort of virtual non-geographical parish made up of those who were not resident in the parish but whose names were entered on the church electoral roll.

The ecclesiastical law of the Church defines the characteristics of parish ministry, and the ordinal assumes that the usual form of ministry will be pastoral: a priest is to work as servant and shepherd among the people to whom he or she has been sent. The ordinal lists the various aspects of this ministry. The priest will:

- proclaim the word of the Lord;
- call those who hear the word to repentance;

- absolve sinners and declare the forgiveness of sins;
- baptize and prepare the baptized for confirmation;
- preside at the celebration of the Holy Communion;
- lead the people in prayer and worship;
- pray for them and bless them;
- teach and encourage them by word and example;
- minister to the sick;
- prepare the dying for death.

The list is not comprehensive and the parish priest will, in addition, promote vocations to lay and ordained ministry, facilitate lay participation in the life of the Church, encourage the incorporation of the baptized into the Church, prepare couples for marriage and celebrate holy matrimony, officiate at funerals and comfort those who mourn, and do many other things as well.

A further insight into the Church's mission in the parish is provided by the description of the functions of the PCC found in the Parochial Church Councils (Powers) Measure 1956. The PCC is to co-operate with the incumbent 'in promoting in the parish the whole mission of the Church, pastoral, evangelistic, social and ecumenical'. The word 'pastoral', deriving from the work of the shepherd, refers to care for all the people of the parish and not just those already engaged in its worshipping life. The second term, 'evangelistic', indicates that mission, the proclamation of the good news of Jesus Christ, is an essential feature of the parish and one that concerns the PCC. The word 'social' has a double meaning. It may refer to encouraging the social life of the parish, providing opportunities for fellowship, but its more significant meaning, in the context of theology, is the social engagement of the Church. The Church of England's website sums up what this means:

> The Church of England's engagement with the public life of people society [*sic*] is an integral part of its calling to live out the Christian faith in England and internationally. It is a central aspect of the vocation of Christians to respond to human need by loving service; to seek to transform unjust structures of society and to strive to safeguard the integrity of creation and renew the life of the earth.[1]

The social mission in a parish must include a commitment to these issues. The final term is 'ecumenical' and indicates the convergence of the Christian traditions and denominations in a common profession of faith and in united service of the community. It is part of our Christian witness in a parish to ensure that the different strands of Christianity are not working in opposition to each other. Within Anglicanism, this must also mean attention to the different approaches encapsulated in our party terms, such as 'catholic' and 'evangelical', 'high', 'low', broad', etc., in order to ensure that our own tradition does not fragment.

The critics of parish ministry see it as limited by geography, by changes in society and, perhaps most significantly, by its lack of an explicit missionary dimension. The report *Mission-Shaped Church* (Church House Publishing, 2004) has an ambivalent attitude to parishes. In the preface, the Bishop of Maidstone writes of the changing nature of community in Britain today. Communities, he says, 'are multi-layered, comprising neighbourhoods, usually with permeable boundaries, and a wide variety of networks, ranging from the relatively local to the global'.[2] He goes on to affirm that the parochial system is essential and central to the delivery of the 'incarnational mission' of the national Church, but that it is also unable 'fully to deliver its mission purpose'. The body of the report, however, states that 'not only are networks more dominant for many people, but parishes are not what they used to be' and goes on to declare that 'only a mixed economy of neighbourhood and network, collaborating together over a wider area (perhaps a deanery), can both adequately fulfil the incarnational principle and demonstrate the universality of Christ's lordship in all expressions of society'.[3] This is a bold and unsubstantiated statement. It may be that a combination of approaches will be more effective in delivering both mission and pastoral care, but the 'new expressions' of church can look like a fad, different for the sake of being different, and attention also needs to be given to the many parishes that work.

The report frequently affirms that 'parish and network are both valid',[4] both necessary if the Church is to serve those who reside in parishes, those who live in neighbourhoods that overlap parishes, and those who 'inhabit networks that are disconnected from the notion of parish or territory'. Nevertheless, it says almost nothing about the way in which the parish can be changed from a sort of 'service centre' concerned essentially with its own members into a focus for Christian communities, nourished by the Eucharist, hearers of the Word, inspired by the Holy Spirit, whose endeavour is to carry out Christ's mission. Its concern is with 'new expressions', but the parish – one of the oldest expressions of the Church – can still be a vital centre of Christian witness and service.

Organization of a parish

What sort of organization is a parish? In terms of categories identified or developed by Mike Hudson, a consultant to not-for-profit organizations and a visiting fellow at the London School of Economics, in his book *Managing Without Profit*,[5] it is a religious organization; its purpose seems to be that of providing mutual support (for those who 'belong' to it) and services (for those who choose to 'use' it); it is largely funded by voluntary donations and its governing body, the PCC, is composed of elected members (those who 'belong' rather than those who 'use'). Such a description is initially helpful in placing the parish as an organization in a wider context, but it is an inadequate description because it says nothing about shared values (other than labelling them as 'religious') or about the environment in which the parish exists or about its structures. The simplest description of a parish centres on its being a Christian community and, as such, its purpose is to follow the commandments of Jesus Christ, namely –

1. To proclaim the good news (gospel) of Jesus Christ and actively to seek to make disciples.
2. To baptize and to work to incorporate the baptized into the life of the Church.
3. To celebrate the Eucharist ('Do this in memory of me') and to be a eucharistically centred community.
4. To be a community characterized by and expressing the love that Jesus had for his disciples.

The creation of PCCs

Many people think that Parochial Church Councils are historic, part of the original structure of the parish. In fact they are less than 100 years old.

In the year after the ending of the Great War, Parliament passed an act entitled the 'Church of England Assembly (Powers) Act 1919', commonly called 'The Enabling Act'. Among its provisions was the establishment of Parochial Church Councils. It also created the National Assembly of the Church of England, known as 'the Church Assembly' (and replaced in 1970 by the General Synod). The act conferred on the new Church Assembly 'powers in regard to legislation touching matters concerning the Church of England' and established the Ecclesiastical Committee of Parliament, consisting of equal numbers of members of the Lords and Commons, to which Church

Assembly measures had to be submitted. A Church Assembly or General Synod Measure, having been laid before Parliament and received the royal assent, has the same force as an Act of Parliament. PCCs themselves came into existence in July 1921, after the passing by the Church Assembly of the Parochial Church Councils (Powers) Measure 1921 'to confer powers on Parochial Church Councils and to amend the law relating to the parochial organisation of the Church of England'. The councils took on most of the powers, duties and liabilities from earlier bodies known as parish vestries, except with regard to the election of churchwardens and sidesmen and some other matters. (The standard nineteenth-century legal textbook by Sir Robert Phillimore, revised for a second edition by his son, Sir Walter Phillimore, and entitled *The Ecclesiastical Law of the Church of England* (1895), described vestries as

> the assembly of the whole parish met together in some convenient place, for the dispatch of the affairs and business of the parish; and this meeting being commonly holden in the vestry adjoining to, or belonging to the church, it thence took the name of vestry, as the place itself does, from the priest's vestments which are usually deposited and kept there.)

The councils also took on the powers, duties and liabilities of the churchwardens of the parish with regard to the financial affairs of the church and the keeping of accounts, the care, maintenance, preservation and insurance of the fabric of the church and of its goods and ornaments, and the care and maintenance of any churchyard. Not every churchman agreed with these developments; according to Dean Inge, Dean of St Paul's, for instance: 'During the miseries of the Great War and the troublous year 1919, a faction of busy-bodies seized the opportunity to agitate for more powers of self-government for the Church.'[6]

Various parts of the 1921 Measure became obsolescent as parishes got used to having PCCs and the powers and responsibilities of other officers and bodies were transferred to them. Coming into operation in 1957, the Representation of the Laity Measure 1956 and the Parochial Church Councils (Powers) Measure 1956 tidied up the piecemeal developments of the various pieces of legislation passed in 1919–22, making a number of amendments and making the measures easier to understand. The Parochial Church Councils (Powers) Measure 1956 is still in force, while the Representation of the Laity Measure has been superseded by the Church Representation Rules (CRRs), the latest edition of which was published in January 2006.

♦ 2 ♦

What is the PCC?

In June 2003 the House of Lords dealt with a case concerning the common law obligation of lay rectors, who need not be members of the Church, to maintain the chancel of the parish church. The opinions of the Lords of Appeal included, among other things, some helpful statements about the PCC.[7] Lord Nicholls of Birkenhead defined a PCC in this way:

> Parochial church councils are established as corporate bodies under a church measure, now the Parochial Church Councils (Powers) Measure 1956. For historical reasons this unique form of legislation, having the same force as a statute, is the way the Church of England governs its affairs. But the essential role of a parochial church council is to provide a formal means, prescribed by the Church of England, whereby ex officio and elected members of the local church promote the mission of the Church and discharge financial responsibilities in respect of their own parish church, including responsibilities regarding maintenance of the fabric of the building.

The Lords had to consider whether a PCC was a public authority and decided it was not. Lord Rodger of Earlsferry said:

> For the most part, in performing his duties and conducting the prescribed services, the minister is simply carrying out part of the mission of the Church, not any governmental function of the state. On the other hand, when in the course of his pastoral duties the minister marries a couple in the parish church, he may be carrying out a governmental function in a broad sense and so may be regarded as a public authority for the purposes of the 1998 [Human Rights] Act. In performing its duties in relation to the maintenance of the fabric of the church so that services may take place there, the PCC is doing its part to help the minister discharge his pastoral and evangelistic duties. The PCC may be acting in the public interest, in a general sense, but it is still carrying out a church rather than a governmental function. That remains the case even although, from time to time, when performing one of his pastoral duties – conducting a marriage service in the church – the minister himself may act as a public authority.

The PCC is a legally constituted entity with specific responsibilities. It may be defined as an elected body or council dealing with finance and organization of the church in a parish or ecclesiastical district of the Church of England.

The Church Representation Rules (CRRs) contain an essential appendix of 'General Provisions Relating to Parochial Church Councils'. This appendix provides information about running the PCC, but does not set down its powers, which can be found in the Parochial Church Councils (Powers) Measure 1956. The Canons of the Church of England provide some further details of the responsibilities and powers of the PCC. PCCs are also subject to the legal rules generally applicable to charities and to the provisions of the Charities Act 1993.

First, though, we have other things to consider before turning to matters of charity and ecclesiastical law.

Is there a spirituality appropriate to the PCC?

The parish is the workshop in which we are to serve Christ. It is, or should be, a form of community centred on the worship in the parish church. As a community, much can be learned from the Rule of St Benedict for monasteries, for the life of a monk is not entirely dissimilar from that of the leaders of a parish community.[8] The intention of all that we do in the parish is the same as that identified in chapter 57 of the Rule, which is concerned with the monastery's craftworkers: *ut in omnibus Deus glorificetur* – 'that in all things God may be glorified'. This should be the intention of the PCC – that God may be glorified in all things in the parish. The legal materials provide a framework: they determine who holds office, how they are elected, the form of meetings, the limits of authority, and so on. They do not provide for the relationships between people or the different roles they play.

The centre of the life of the ecclesiastical parish is the parish church – or, rather, the worship that takes place in that church or other building used for worship. Worship comes before mission or teaching, and the purpose of worship is not to make us feel good – it is to glorify God. So whatever form it takes, our worship should be fit for that purpose. Around this centre of worship there will be many other parish activities undertaken in other places and by a variety of people – the PCC meeting, work in the parish office, the playgroup, the church school, the old people's lunch club, the children's after school club, the coffee morning, the confirmation class, and so on. There should be no real separation between the parish's worship and anything else that goes on; in all things God should be glorified. Our attitude should be the same whether we serve at the altar or mow the churchyard grass, play in the music group or collect the elderly for a midweek service. St Benedict's Rule urges an attitude of careful attention to whatever is at hand, and linked to this is the idea that one activity should not be held more worthy of this careful attention than any other. This is a difficult habit to acquire, and is not limited to church matters. Every task we face, no matter how humble, mundane or frequent, is a job in which God can be glorified. In his hymn 'New every morning is the love', John Keble wrote:

> If on our daily course our mind
> Be set to hallow all we find,
> New treasures still, of countless price,
> God will provide for sacrifice.
>
> We need not bid, for cloistered cell,
> Our neighbour and our work farewell,
> Nor strive to wind ourselves too high
> For sinful man beneath the sky.
>
> The trivial round, the common task,
> Would furnish all we ought to ask, –
> Room to deny ourselves, a road
> To bring us daily nearer God.[9]

Here is a straightforward expression of a spirituality consonant with that of St Benedict. If our attitude is such that we want to offer to God everything we do, everything that comes to us in a day, then from those things will come the treasures to be offered to God. And we do not need to be monks or nuns to achieve this, nor should we think that such an attitude is possible only if we strive for higher spiritual levels. Keble is concerned with everyday living, with the trivial round and the common task. These will give us all we need, setting us on the road that brings us daily nearer God, with every day providing a new opportunity for doing this. So, it is not just what we do 'for the Church' that is significant, but everything that we do, and the offering of our work to God needs to be habitual.

To achieve this attitude, our day – the day we are offering to God – needs some shape. The monastic day has a rhythm of working hours, prayer and recreation. Each of the ingredients receives full attention. The shape of our day is frequently generated by other people and their needs, or by our having to go off to work somewhere;

but even into these days we can, with flexibility, introduce the elements of prayer and recreation. At its simplest, the prayer part might be saying the psalms set for the day in the Book of Common Prayer, before breakfast (or on the train or wherever) and before bed. If we want some richer fare, we can always use the daily office in one of its many accessible forms. The purpose in this gentle discipline is the cultivation of an attitude that does not divide what we do for the Church from what we do for anyone else. The idea is to live for God, and in so living to do something that might affect the world in which we are living and working, by bringing to it some glimmer of the light of Christ. And if we are not serving the world, how can we serve the parish?

Wil Derkse, author of *The Rule of Benedict for Beginners: Spirituality for Daily Life* (Liturgical Press, 2003), tells of his regular visits to a Benedictine monastery and his gradual growth in Benedictine spirituality, not as something in which he was merely interested but as something to which he was committed. When he entered into a more committed relationship by becoming an oblate – someone outside a monastery who is attuned to the life of the community – he identified three specific areas of attention. First, joining in the daily office; second, daily prayerful reading; third, modelling daily living in accordance with the three monastic vows. These are not poverty, chastity and obedience, but *stabilitas, conversatio morum* and *obedientia. Stabilitas* means not running away from whatever is at hand and to which you are committed; it means holding on joyfully, with perseverance and patience. It involves commitment to growth where you are, where you are planted. *Conversatio morum*, generally and obscurely translated as 'conversation of manners', means a permanent process dedicated to changing one's attitude and lifestyle for the better; it is directed to our values, and to the habits that are consonant with those values. *Obedientia*, often thought of as obedience, even blind obedience, to the Rule, means the art of very careful listening and responding – the discerning listening of the heart.

Following Derkse, let us apply some of the lessons of the Rule to the PCC, beginning with leadership. The minister, churchwardens and other members of the PCC are leaders of the parish community, charged with the task of working together to promote the whole mission of the Church. Derkse says that leadership should be conferred on people who have a special talent for careful listening and responding. He points to the chapters of the Rule concerned with the abbot, the cellarer and the prior, all of which offer good advice for people in positions of responsibility. The key is flexibility in handling people –

a flexibility that takes account of differences in talents, and levels of human and spiritual development. The abbot is to 'so arrange everything that the strong have something still to wish for and the weak nothing from which to shrink'. It is very important, Derkse notes, to attend to the weak, and to difficult people, but careful attention to the strong and talented is equally important and easily forgotten. The PCC too must attend to the needs of the strong within its own number, as well as nurturing both weak and strong within the parish.

Often the PCC has to make decisions, and here again careful listening is essential. The more important the decision, the wider the circle of those to whom one should listen. The Rule says this: 'Whenever any important matters have to be settled in the monastery, the abbot should call together the whole community and explain what is to be discussed. After he has heard the brethren's advice, he should reflect upon it, then do what he judges best.' There are three aspects involved: listening, taking to heart, responding by appropriate action. First the leader explains what is to be discussed, showing that he or she has a clear understanding of the situation, then listens, then takes time to reflect – and only then acts.

This must, of course, be a genuine process of listening and reflection. It is pointless and frustrating to others involved if the leader makes a decision, then consults, then ignores anything that is contrary to the decision already made. It is expected today that bodies, such as the disciplinary tribunals of professional bodies, for example, will give the reasons for the decisions that have been made, so that people can understand the process that produced the result. Here are two scenarios for the appointment of a new rural dean:

First scenario

The bishop wrote to all the deanery clergy to inform them that the rural dean was leaving his parish later in the year and that, in order to facilitate a handover period, he was now seeking nominations for the office of rural dean and these were to be received by him within a fortnight. A number of clergy wrote to the bishop immediately, but when the deanery chapter met, the whole process was challenged: there was no job description or person specification, no indication of the time commitment or of the support that the diocese would provide, so how was it possible to nominate? The chapter clerk was asked to express these views to the bishop, but there was no time for a full consultation before the bishop went away on study leave. The clergy received a letter thanking them for their views and naming the new rural dean, but it was not clear what views had been expressed and how the bishop had reached his decision. The senior clergy of the deanery privately expressed their dismay at the appointment.

Second scenario

The bishop wrote to all the deanery clergy to inform them that the rural dean was leaving his parish later in the year and that, in order to facilitate a handover period, he was now seeking nominations for the office of rural dean. He enclosed a job description, drawn up with the assistance of the present dean, a person specification, an indication that the position required one to one-and-a-half days per week to be spent on deanery business, and an assurance that the diocese would meet administrative costs, including a fixed sum towards secretarial expenses. The bishop asked for a swift response to his consultation because he was going on study leave in a fortnight. Shortly after the consultation period ended, the bishop wrote again to the clergy to say that 12 out of 16 of the deanery clergy had responded to his invitation. A variety of views had been expressed but they divided into two basic positions, favouring either one of the more senior clergy of the deanery, a team rector with over 10 years' service, or one of the younger incumbents, serving in a parish which had the support of a number of retired clergy and readers. The bishop had sounded out both candidates and reached the conclusion, after considering the current needs of the deanery, that the younger candidate should be appointed on this occasion. The deanery clergy were content with the appointment.

In the first scenario the consultation appears to be a formality. No one except the bishop knows how many clergy wrote to him or the thrust of what they said. It is not clear whether he took note of their comments, or simply appointed the person he had first thought of. In the second scenario the bishop has taken the trouble to show that he had a clear grasp of the situation (he issued a job description and person specification), that he asked for views and listened to them, that he reflected on what he heard, and then acted in a way that was both transparent and accountable. The keywords are 'take the trouble'. Genuine listening takes time and trouble.

Two further things should be noted here. First, the decision-making process within the Benedictine tradition is not, as we might say, democratic, but consultation nevertheless plays a major part. There is no voting, but the leader, presiding over the community, listens attentively before reaching a decision. Some decisions taken in the parish might be reached in a similar way, taken by the responsible person after proper consultation, rather than being determined by a majority vote. Second, even when decisions are made by voting in a PCC meeting, they should be preceded by attentive listening. Everyone present needs to listen. Conversely, everyone who has something to say needs to speak and to do so as clearly and concisely as they are able. What often happens is that people arrive at a meeting with minds already made up, with a position taken and arguments in support of that position. Often participants do not listen to what others are saying, but are just waiting for the moment to have their own say and to undermine the arguments of another person. One consequence of attentive listening is that meetings may take longer, and that non-urgent decisions may need to be put off to another day in order to allow reflection on what has been heard.

Personality type

From our conversations with many clergy and PCC members, we are aware that PCCs are often subject to misunderstandings and conflicts. These sometimes arise because of personality type. At its most basic, it may be about the way in which we make decisions. The much used Myers-Briggs Type Indicator™ divides people into Extravert (E) and Introvert (I). A study of personality type and religious leadership[10] indicated some differences between the types that are relevant to decision-making (see Table 2.1).

Table 2.1 Differences between extraverts and introverts

Extravert	*Introvert*
Interested in external happenings	Interested in internal reactions
Energized by contact with large numbers of people	Fatigued by contact with large numbers of people
Fatigued by steady reading or study: needs breaks to talk to people	Energized by reading, meditating, study
Opens mouth; then engages brain	Engages brain; then may or may not open mouth
Leaves wishing he or she hadn't said it	Leaves wishing he or she had said it
Action and practical achievement	Ideas and abstract invention
Breadth	Depth
Talkative, active	Reserved, reflective
Using trial and error with confidence	Considering deeply before acting

---

Scenario

PCC meetings in a particular parish were often difficult. The vicar and churchwardens worked closely together, talked often and sorted out their plans and proposals for the PCC but, as they urged action on any matter, so the majority of PCC members resisted them. After going on a Myers-Briggs workshop, the vicar understood that he and the churchwardens were introverts. They took the time to consider a course of action, and when they were ready they presented it to the PCC and expected a decision. But the PCC had a majority of introverts who also needed time to reach a decision and almost always deferred action to the next meeting. The vicar and churchwardens set about increasing the amount of time members had to review their proposals, and it all started to work much more smoothly.

The Myers-Briggs Type Indicator™ is not a panacea for all ills in the PCC, but it does suggest that we may be able to listen more willingly and to act more effectively when we understand the needs of different personality types.

Murmuratio

Careful listening, consultation, cheerfulness and a good word are antidotes to the poison of *murmuratio*. Murmuring – the nit-picking, grumbling, complaining atmosphere that can be generated within a community – is a slow-working poison that corrodes vision, saps intellectual and moral energy, and eats away at the heart of a community. Sometimes the murmurers will not cease from their murmuring, and action must be taken – not as punishment, but as a way of promoting improvement and growth. The responsibility for dealing with murmuring rests on the whole leadership, on the whole PCC. All too frequently both minister and PCC hear the concerns of the most anxious, cynical and passive-aggressive people in the community, and will be caught up in trying to please or pacify them. A disproportionate amount of time, energy and resources gets tied up in this, and it is not in the best interests of the parish. If the PCC learns to listen and to respond constructively and appropriately, setting boundaries on how emerging issues will be addressed (and testing if a matter really is 'an issue'), then it should become increasingly possible to focus on real concerns.

PCC members need to learn to speak for themselves, to say not 'people are saying' but 'I am saying', and to discourage the 'manipulative confidentiality' that poisons the community. We mean by this the way in which a PCC member, reporting a complaint to the churchwardens or the minister, refuses to identify the person who made the complaint, claiming: 'I was told in confidence.' This is using confidentiality as a weapon. When someone comes bearing the message of an invisible group, then the PCC needs to respond by asking: 'Who is saying this? Let us meet them and listen to them.'

> St Paul: *Do all things without murmurings and disputings.*
> [Philippians 2.14]

The PCC needs to adopt a process of testing to enable the whole community to cope with the few persistent voices that press a concern, complaint or idea affecting the community's life. It is not a process to be used often, but without it there can be no sound judgement. If the members of the PCC perceive that there is a real and significant concern, then it can arrange to meet with parishioners, formally or informally, to listen. Someone, perhaps the minister, might first set out the PCC's concerns, suggesting that there is no right or wrong response, stressing that members wish to know what the community thinks. Having listened, the PCC members can reflect together on what has been heard, and decide what action is necessary. The PCC will achieve this only if the members have individually and collectively focused on listening as a necessary skill and a characteristic feature of PCC meetings. Robert A. Gallagher, the founder of the Church Development Institute program in the United States,[11] writes that parishes using Benedictine principles need:

1 Listening and problem solving processes. Ways in which people can express new ideas, suggestions for improvements, concerns and problems. Parishes need processes for hearing and addressing issues.
2 A 'no grumbling' norm. We need to ask people to honour each other and the well-being of the community. If the community has ways to listen and to work together in improving its common life, members need to be asked to use that process. There needs to be an explicit invitation to exercise self-discipline over what and how we speak in addressing issues and especially when things don't go our way.

3 To train and support leaders in their ministry with chronic grumblers as well as those who are especially insistent around a particular issue. Train leaders in how to: listen to upset or anxious members, explain the parish's position, and invite people to participate without trying to take responsibility for convincing people. Have leaders learn to be firm in inviting members to offer their concerns and ideas in the community's normal processes for channelling and testing rather than have the leader accept responsibility for the members' issue.[12]

Speaking of the Rule of St Benedict, Archbishop Rowan Williams said that:

> Everyone in the community that the Rule envisages is responsible both to and for everyone else in different modes, depending on the different specific responsibilities they hold, but nonetheless sharing a single basic calling in this respect . . . The workshop is manifestly a collaborative venture with the aim of 'mending vices and preserving love' . . . the workshop is at the end of the day a solid and tough metaphor for that spirituality which is a lifetime's labour, yet also an expansion of the heart.[13]

He meant, first, that everyone within the community has a responsibility *to* the community and *for* the community. The degree and type of responsibility varies because people hold different offices, but these offices are held *within* the community. So everyone in the PCC has a responsibility *within* the parish community, *to* the parish community and *for* the parish community, for there is a single basic calling to serve Christ in and for the parish. The 'workshop' to which Benedict refers is the monastery; the PCC's workshop is the parish. The fruitfulness of the Church's mission in the parish depends upon collaboration between clergy and laity. But the Archbishop's second point is that the effectiveness of our labour in the workshop depends upon our discipleship, upon the way in which we grow spiritually and our ability to bring this genuine spirituality to bear on the work of the parish. 'Mending vices' may here mean addressing, among other things, sloth (failure to do what we have agreed to do) and anger (at those with whom we cannot agree). 'Preserving love' means working to ensure that the church and parish is a community in which the disciples of Christ love each other as Christ loves them.

A PCC will need to deal with matters in a way that respects the laws civil and ecclesiastical, complies with regulations, and discharges its obligations effectively and efficiently, and it must do all these things in a way that is profoundly Christian. One godly bishop described church administration as the 'housekeeping of the household of God'. It is an apt description because it shows that, even when we are dealing with tasks that can seem very remote from the Christian mission, we are engaged in an essentially Christian task. The spirituality of the PCC should undergird and facilitate the exercise of its legal responsibilities, to which we must now turn.

The PCC as a body corporate

The third clause of the Parochial Church Councils (Powers) Measure 1956 defines the corporate nature of the PCC:

> Every council shall be a body corporate by the name of the parochial church council of the parish for which it is appointed and shall have perpetual succession. Any act of the council may be signified by an instrument executed pursuant to a resolution of the council and under the hands or if an instrument under seal is required under the hands and seal of the chairman presiding and two other members of the council present at the meeting at which such resolution is passed.

The Charity Commission defines a body corporate as a

> collection of persons which, in the eyes of the law, has its own legal existence (and rights and duties) separate from those of the persons who form it from time to time. It has a name or title of its own and may also have a common seal for use on official documents.[14]

The Commission states further that 'The PCC is a body corporate with perpetual succession, but without a common seal'.[15] The term 'shall have perpetual succession' means that the existence of the council does not depend on the existence of its members – that is, members may change or die, but the body corporate continues to exist.

Personal liability

People often worry about whether they will be personally liable if the PCC finds itself in financial difficulties, faced with a bill which normal church funds cannot cover. Provided the PCC has acted legally and followed the correct procedures, the answer is 'No'.

The individual members of the PCC are responsible for the management of the body corporate, but the duties, responsibilities and liabilities lie with the body corporate itself. There are circumstances, however, in which an individual member becomes liable. This is when an officer or member of the PCC has initiated an action or made a commitment that is contrary to PCC policy or which contravenes some regulation that affects the PCC's ability to act. That officer or member may be held liable to the PCC for any liability that it has itself incurred because of the breach of trust. For example, a member might be personally liable if he or she made a fraudulent or negligent statement which resulted in loss to a third party.

As Judge Quentin Edwards QC said in his judgement in the Chichester Consistory Court (re St Thomas à Becket, Framfield, September 1987) ([1989] 1 WLR 689, [1989] 1 All ER 170):

> A parochial church council is a body corporate (see s.3 of the Parochial Church Councils (Powers) Measure 1956), and therefore no individual member of a council is personally liable for any debt or other liability of the body corporate which has been lawfully incurred. If, however, works to a church are executed without due authority, and so unlawfully, by the direction of a churchwarden or other member of the council that protection is lost.

Charitable status

A PCC is the trustee body of an excepted charity.[16] It is the PCC, not the individual members, that is the trustee. Acting in the corporate capacity as trustees, the members of the PCC must act reasonably and prudently in all matters relating to the charity and always act in its best interests. Certain charities are exempt from registration with the Charity Commission because they are considered to be adequately supervised by, or accountable to, some other body or authority. They fall into three main groups: those excepted from registration by Order or Regulation of the Home Secretary or the Charity Commission, very small charities (with an annual income of £1,000 or less, and without endowment or property), and registered places of worship. The 13,000 PCCs of the Church of England are excepted from registration by Statutory Instrument.

Limited exception from registration was conferred upon PCCs by the now revoked 1963 Regulations (of the Charity Commission). The Commission subsequently concluded that PCCs are established for exclusively charitable purposes and are charities within the meaning of the 1993 Charities Act. PCCs are excepted from registration under regulation 4(2)(b) of the 1996 Regulations; this exception runs until 1 October 2007 and applies whatever the income level of the PCC. PCCs are considered to be 'bodies wholly or mainly concerned with the advancement of religion, connected with the Church of England, and established wholly or mainly to make provision for public worship.'[17]

Excepted charities are subject to the legal rules generally applicable to charities and to the provisions of the Charities Act 1993, but are not required to register with the Charity Commission (though they may do so if they wish), but they enjoy the status and the fiscal benefits (such as Gift Aid) accorded to other charities. For PCCs, the principal effect of the Charities Act 1993 concerns the accounting regulations.

The Cabinet Office's Strategy Unit report 'Private Action, Public Benefit' proposed the abolition of excepted charities and a requirement to register for any charity with an income in excess of £50,000. In response, in December 2002 the Archbishops' Council urged a registration threshold of £100,000, pointing out that if it was to be £50,000 then 3,800 to 4,500 parishes would need to register, while if it was over £100,000 it would affect around 1,700 parishes (depending on which year the Act comes into force). It is clear from the Charities Bill currently (i.e. as at September 2006) before Parliament that this recommendation of the Archbishops' Council has been accepted.

♦ 3 ♦

Specific responsibilities of the PCC

The responsibilities of the PCC, as laid down in the Parochial Church Councils (Powers) Measure 1956, are:

- to care for, maintain, preserve and take out adequate insurance cover for the fabric, goods and ornaments of the church;
- to agree a budget and to be responsible for the income and expenditure of the parish;
- to maintain proper financial records and accounting procedures;
- to prepare annual financial statements and an annual report, and present them to the Annual Parochial Church Meeting (APCM);
- to arrange for independent examination or audit of the financial statements;
- to care for and maintain the churchyard;
- to consult with the incumbent on matters of general concern and importance to the parish;
- to co-operate with the incumbent in promoting the mission of the Church.

We will now examine each of these responsibilities in turn, as well as discussing the PCC as employer and touching on those areas which are *not* the responsibility of the PCC.

To care for, maintain, preserve and take out adequate insurance cover for the fabric, goods and ornaments of the church

Though the Care of Churches and Ecclesiastical Jurisdiction Measure 1991 (Section 5) lays overall responsibility for the fabric on the churchwardens, members of the PCC are also charged with its care, maintenance, preservation and insurance. Canon F 14, 'Of the provision of things appertaining to churches', states that everything a church needs, and all the obligations for care and repair of churches, chapels and churchyards shall be 'provided and performed . . . by and at the charge of the parochial church council'.

Faculties

PCC members need to understand the basics of faculty jurisdiction, as it is through a resolution of the PCC that incumbent and churchwardens are authorized to apply for a faculty – that is, authorization of works in and alterations to the fabric and contents of churches, and to churchyards.

The obligation as set out in the Care of Churches and Ecclesiastical Jurisdiction Measure 1991 and the Faculty Jurisdiction Rules 2000 is that a faculty must be secured before any work or alterations are carried out to a church or its furnishings, or in the churchyard or curtilage, or before anything is introduced into or removed from a church. A faculty is granted, or refused, by the chancellor of the diocese (a professional judge and the bishop's chief legal officer).

Most diocesan chancellors issue a list – known as the *de minimis* list – of works that may be carried out without a faculty. Such a list is specific to a given diocese and may vary from time to time. In general, such a list is likely to include:

1 Works of routine maintenance on the fabric (up to a certain value and after consultation with the archdeacon), on electrical fittings and equipment, and on furniture.
2 Movables (cruets, vases, surplices, cassocks, vergers' robes, authorized service books, Bibles, hymnbooks, replacement altar linen, temporary banners, replacement of worn-out flags, temporary items of decoration, such as Christmas trees).
3 Furniture and fixtures in church halls, kitchens and toilets, fire extinguishers, replacement of carpets and curtains originally introduced by faculty.
4 Routine tuning of organs and pianos.
5 Bells: certain repairs to bellropes, pulleys, bearings, stays, etc.
6 Inspection and routine maintenance of clocks.
7 Purchase and maintenance of lawnmowers.
8 Certain items of work that may be authorized by the archdeacon.

The current diocesan list should always be referred to (they are often available on diocesan websites) and the archdeacon or diocesan registrar consulted if there is any doubt about whether a matter requires a faculty.

In granting a faculty the chancellor takes into consideration the advice of the Diocesan Advisory Committee (DAC), to whom the proposal and plans must be submitted before the faculty application is made. (The DAC advises the chancellor, not the parish, but most

DACs nevertheless welcome early consultation about significant alterations to ensure that there are no difficulties with the formal submission.) When a proposal is put formally to the DAC it has to include:

1 Full details of the proposed work.
2 Plans, designs and specifications.
3 An estimate of the cost.
4 The comments of the inspecting architect.
5 The name of the architect employed (if not the inspecting architect).
6 Details of all contractors.
7 Photographs of the church.
8 Photographs of any items to be introduced into or removed from the church.

When a proposal concerns an organ, bells or a clock, the papers are referred to a diocesan adviser for evaluation.

(The 'inspecting architect', or 'quinquennial inspector', is the architect or surveyor who undertakes the quinquennial inspection of the church building once every five years. He or she is chosen by the PCC, but the appointment must be approved by the DAC.)

The DAC, after due consideration, returns the plans and other documents to the applicants (usually marked with the DAC's stamp), and the committee's certificate relating to the proposals. The certificate sets out the works considered by the DAC and gives the committee's recommendation. It can recommend, not recommend, or raise no objection. The second part of the certificate comments on the effect the proposals will have on the historical or archaeological significance of the building and advises on consultation with English Heritage, the local planning authority, National Amenity Societies, the Council for the Care of Churches and other persons or bodies.

Equipped with the DAC certificate, the minister and churchwardens as petitioners can now proceed to a petition for the faculty. Where the PCC will have come into the process is in authorizing the minister and churchwardens to make this petition, after having been consulted on the proposal and plans for the work and agreeing that it should go ahead, subject to DAC advice and faculty permission. A faculty can be sought even if the DAC does not recommend it be granted, but it cannot be sought without PCC agreement. The application (or 'petition') to the chancellor must include a certified copy of the resolution by the PCC relating to the works and proposals. The public notice part of the petition must be displayed outside the church, where it can be read by members of the public, for a period of 28 days before the petition is sent to the diocesan registrar (the legal adviser to the bishop and the diocese).

This is the information the minister and churchwardens will need for every faculty petition:

1. The date of the church.
2. If it is listed, its grade.
3. Information about whether it is or adjoins an ancient monument or is in a conservation area or a national park.
4. The name of the inspecting architect or surveyor.
5. The name of the architect or surveyor engaged for the works.
6. A statement of the cost of the works.
7. Details of the way in which the cost will be met, including the terms of any grant or offer of a grant.
8. Confirmation that other consents (planning authority, scheduled monument consent) have been obtained.
9. Information about bats. (Do you have them? Will the proposals affect them? Have you taken advice from English Nature?)
10. Details of contractors.
11. Timing of the work.
12. Arrangements if the church is to be closed.
13. A PCC resolution.
14. A DAC certificate.

The other information required will depend on the sort of building you are dealing with and the sort of work you are proposing to do.

A number of the cases in ecclesiastical law reported in the journal of the Ecclesiastical Law Society and also now posted on the Society's website at <http://www.ecclawsoc.org.uk> has concerned work undertaken without a faculty. Chancellor Bursell in the Durham Consistory Court (re St Giles, Durham, October 1998) reminded the parties, seeking a confirmatory faculty (i.e. a faculty to approve work already carried out) for various unauthorized works to a Grade I listed building (construction of a path and access ramp, the sanding of a wooden floor, alterations to pews, and the painting of the pulpit, altar rails, roof beams and corbels) of the provisions of Canon F 13 and stated that 'because the Church of England and therefore its officers such as the minister and churchwardens are trustees of the heritage of the parish, the diocese and the nation, ignorance of the law and even well-intentioned breaches of the law cannot and will not be tolerated'. The PCC was ordered to pay the court fees.

Chancellor Coningsby, in the York Consistory Court (re All Saints, North Street, September 1999), was also concerned with works undertaken in a Grade I listed church, during restoration after a fire. Some work was undertaken that was not covered by the original faculty, including removal of a piece of a medieval pillar, and the petitioners sought a confirmatory faculty. The chancellor was 'critical of the churchwardens, PCC and parish architect for proceeding without authority of a faculty' and when he granted the faculty he ordered all the court and registry costs to be borne by the petitioners. Chancellor Coningsby was acting with the same intent as the Chancellor of Chichester, Judge Quentin Edwards QC, in the Chichester Consistory Court (re St Thomas à Becket, Framfield, September 1987) ([1989] 1 WLR 689, [1989] 1 All ER 170). In his judgement (part of which we quoted earlier), he said:

> The churchwardens, and their successors in that office, are not, as lay men and women, liable to such proceedings [under the Ecclesiastical Jurisdiction Measure 1963]. They, however, should appreciate the pecuniary risks which they will run should they ever again execute such works without authority. A parochial church council is a body corporate (see s.3 of the Parochial Church Councils (Powers) Measure 1956), and therefore no individual member of a council is personally liable for any debt or other liability of the body corporate which has been lawfully incurred. If, however, works to a church are executed without due authority, and so unlawfully, by the direction of a churchwarden or other member of the council that protection is lost. If, therefore, a churchwarden, acting alone or with others, directs works to a church without the authority of an archdeacon's certificate or faculty he may expose himself to grave financial liability and loss. He may be ordered, personally, to pay the costs incurred in obtaining a confirmatory faculty. The archdeacon may himself seek a faculty authorising the undoing or alteration of the works and if such faculty be granted to the archdeacon the churchwarden may be ordered to pay all the archdeacon's costs and expenses, viz. both his legal costs and the costs of the remedial works.

It is essential that PCC members understand the part they play with regard to the care of churches and the faculty jurisdiction and, if they – or their churchwardens – are to avoid legal penalties, follow the rules exactly.

Insurance

There is no obligation in ecclesiastical law to insure the church building. Nevertheless, trustees have a general duty to protect the property of their charity, and this means that it should be adequately insured against the consequences of misfortune, whether natural, accidental or deliberate. Some types of insurance, such as employer's liability, are required by law.

To agree a budget and to be responsible for the income and expenditure of the parish

The Parochial Church Councils (Powers) Measure 1956 identifies three financial powers of the PCC:

1 Power to frame an annual budget of moneys required for the maintenance of the Church in the parish and otherwise and to take such steps as they think necessary for the raising, collecting and allocating of such moneys.
2 Power to make levy and collect a voluntary church rate for any purpose connected with the affairs of the church including the administrative expenses of the council and the costs of any legal proceedings.
3 Power jointly with the minister to determine the objects to which all moneys to be given or collected in church shall be allocated.

Budget

A budget is, in brief, a financial plan for the short term, typically for one year. More fully, it is a short-term plan that seeks to work towards the achievement of a long-term plan, and an 'estimate of the resources required to achieve a strategy designed to fulfil the objectives of the organisation'.[18]

By itself, a budget statement does not tell you anything. It needs a context. A parish begins with a plan, setting out its purpose, its long- or medium-term objectives, and the means, the strategy or tactics, it will use to achieve its objectives. It then asks about the physical resources – buildings, personnel and money – needed for the purpose, and from this we get the budget – an estimate of financial resources needed. The draft of the budget will identify what is needed to do the minimum – in the case of a parish, for example, to pay the parish share and the minister's expenses and to maintain the church building – and then what more could be done if more financial resources were available. A budget covers one year, but a parish might reasonably consider financial forecasts for future years.

Table 3.1 A budget timetable

Month	*Action*	*Person or body*
September	Identify objectives for the following financial year	Treasurer and Minister
	Prepare draft budget	Treasurer
October	Submit budget to Standing Committee	Treasurer and Standing Committee
	Reconsider objectives etc., if necessary	Treasurer and Minister
November	Submit revised version to PCC	Treasurer
	Further revision in the light of PCC response	Treasurer and Minister or Standing Committee or Budget Working Group
January	Submit final version to PCC	Treasurer

The budget, produced by the treasurer in consultation with the minister and others, will need to be agreed by the PCC prior to or early in the financial year. The Church's financial year is the calendar year. A budget timetable might look like the one shown in Table 3.1.

If the budget is rejected, then it will be necessary for the PCC to reconsider its mission, objectives and strategies in the light of available resources.

An alternative to this process of evaluating objectives and desired outcomes alongside resources – known as preparing a rational budget – is a process of basing the budget on historic levels or patterns of spending; this produces a historic budget. Most parishes, and other charities, use the historic approach most of the time, but every so many years – probably every five years – the budget should be rationally prepared as part of the process of reviewing the parish's mission, objectives and strategies.

In any year the PCC will want to know how income and expenditure are doing in comparison with the budget. The key budgetary control questions are: how are we doing? how much is left? and, how will the year-end look? A budget has a profile which tells us how the predicted income varies through the year. For instance, if the parish holds a summer fair, the profile will show that the money comes in during the sixth or seventh month of the year. If there are 20 weddings in the year and only four of them are in the period January to April, eight are in May to August, and six in September, then the profile will show the income expected in each period. Without the profile, the May PCC meeting may be horrified that income is down. With it, the PCC will know to expect considerable income in the summer months. If, as in so many parishes, the year is back-ended, with significant income from carol and Christmas services, this too needs to be indicated.

If there is a significant variance between the budget figure and actual performance, then the PCC needs to investigate the variance, identify the cause, recalculate as necessary, consider the likely year-end position, and act accordingly (see Figure 7.1 on p. 100).

Voluntary church rate

The PCC has the power to make, levy and collect a voluntary church rate. The publication *The Layman in Church Government* observed that

> in the old days a compulsory church rate similar to the present local authority rate could be levied, but this is no longer possible. The position now is that a rate may be levied, but the ratepayer is under no obligation to pay it unless he wishes to do so.[19]

According to the old law, rates for reparation of the church were to be made by churchwardens, together with the parishioners, duly assembled, after due notice, in the vestry or the church. Because of its place of meeting, the council of an ecclesiastical parish was called the vestry, consisting of the incumbent (minister) and persons of both sexes who were rated to the general rate in respect of the parish, whether resident or not.

The Compulsory Church Rate Abolition Act 1868 effectively abolished compulsory church rates by its first section which stated: 'No suit shall be instituted or proceeding taken in any ecclesiastical or other court or before any justice or magistrate, to enforce or compel the payment of any church rate made in any parish or place in England or Wales.' The Act did not affect the existence of vestries or 'the making, assessing, receiving, or otherwise dealing with any church rate, save in so far as it relates to the recovery thereof'. As we have noted earlier, the Parochial Church Councils (Powers) Measure 1921 transferred the powers of the vestry to the newly established Parochial Church Council.

The 1868 Act, which is still in force, states in Section 7 that:

> It shall be lawful for all bodies corporate, trustees, guardians, and committees who or whose *cestuis que trust* are in the occupation of any

> lands, houses, or tenements, to pay, if they think fit, any church rate made in respect of such property, although the payment of the same may not be enforceable after the passing of this act, and the same shall be allowed to them in any accounts to be rendered by them respectively.

The voluntary church rate is, therefore, a rate rather than a donation, albeit a voluntary one, and can be accounted for as such.

Raising, collecting and allocating moneys

The PCC has the power to take steps to raise, collect and allocate moneys. The PCC will not be starting from scratch – there will be Sunday collections, special collections, planned giving and Gift Aid in place, together with a range of fund-raising events and activities. With a particular objective in mind for a given year, the PCC may also be applying for grants from English Heritage, the Historic Churches Preservation Trust, and other bodies. There is always the possibility of a legacy or some other windfall, which the PCC can allocate for immediate or future use. It may be guided by the minister, the treasurer, the standing committee or a finance committee.

There was a change between the 1921 and 1956 Measures about the allocation of moneys given to the church. The Book of Common Prayer contains this rubric (at the end of the order for Holy Communion): 'After the Divine service ended, the money given at the Offertory shall be disposed of to such pious and charitable uses, as the Minister and Church-wardens shall think fit. Wherein if they disagree, it shall be disposed of as the Ordinary shall appoint.'

If this direction remained in force (as it did in the 1921 Measure), then the money given at every celebration of the Eucharist would go into a fund administered by the minister and churchwardens and would not be part of the income of the PCC. As the Eucharist grew in popularity as the main Sunday service, so more income passed out of the control of the PCC. The 1956 Measure changed this, and money given at the Eucharist is income due to the PCC, to be allocated jointly with the minister.

Example

The bishop was coming to confirm and to preside at the Eucharist. The standard instructions said that the collection at the service was to be paid to the Bishop's Discretionary Fund. The churchwarden, a barrister, noticed this and pointed out that it contravened the Measure and Canon

B17A, which states that the money collected at Holy Communion belongs to the general funds of the PCC. At the PCC meeting it was noted that the costs of the service – i.e. paying the organist and verger – still had to be met, whether or not the bishop was presiding. Someone else pointed out that the bishop came only once every three years, and perhaps some money could be donated to his Fund every year, instead of the three-yearly Confirmation collection. This was agreed and included in the budget.

Canon F 10 stipulates that there shall be an alms box in every church, and that alms so collected are to be 'applied to such uses as the minister and parochial church council shall think fit'. If they can't agree, then they have to ask the bishop to determine the matter.

The task of counting the collection is specifically the responsibility of the churchwardens, to be undertaken in conjunction with the sidesmen. The PCC will nevertheless have some responsibility for this, as it forms part of 'raising and collecting moneys'. It should be ensured that two people count the collections (cash and planned-giving or Gift Aid envelopes) as soon as possible after the services in which they are taken. Preferably the two people doing the counting should not be related to one another; they should not be the same two every week, and they should not always include the treasurer. (These measures are intended to minimize the possibility of fraud or theft – or even the possibility of the suspicion of such things.) The income details should be recorded in the service register and initialled by the counters. The amount in each envelope should also be recorded on the envelope or on a separate sheet; the envelopes (and record sheet if used) should be passed to the stewardship secretary. The money should be banked as soon as possible, and left in the safe until it is banked.

All bank accounts should require two signatures on cheques and other instructions. In order to make the signing of cheques not too long-drawn-out a process, it is worth having at least four signatories (on the basis that at least two of them will generally be available when needed). There is no need for the incumbent or any other member of the clergy to be a signatory, though there is also no prohibition from their being one. A PCC resolution will be needed whenever you need to change bank signatories, and the list of signatories should be reviewed regularly.

Where financial matters are delegated to a member of the church staff, it must be remembered that the PCC retains the legal responsibility for the finances of the parish, and may only delegate financial tasks if it can ensure that its wishes will be followed.

To maintain proper financial records and accounting procedures

PCCs must follow the regulations set out in the Church Accounting Regulations 1997 and the Church Accounting (Amendments) Regulations 2001.

It has been the general policy of the Government to make PCCs accountable in the same way that registered charities are. The requirements are summarized in the important document *The Charities Act 1993 and the PCC* (second edition, 2001).

The accounting records which are maintained on a day-to-day basis (from which the annual financial statements will be prepared and which must be sufficient to show and explain all the PCC's transactions) must be preserved for at least six years from the end of the financial year to which they relate.

To prepare annual financial statements and an annual report, and present them to the Annual Parochial Church Meeting

The powers conferred by the constitution of the National Assembly of the Church of England (1919) as varied by the Representation of the Laity Measure 1929 included the preparation of an annual report, including a report on financial affairs, and its submission to the annual meeting, and the fixing of the date and time of the annual meeting. The requirement for accounts and other reports was laid down in the eighth clause of the Parochial Church Councils (Powers) Measure 1921, which also changed the Church's financial year to have it end on 31 December.

All PCC members need to understand the council's obligations. Those concerning annual accounts, reports and scrutiny are contained in the document just referred to entitled *The Charities Act 1993 and the PCC*. This provides the guidance needed for a PCC to be fully compliant with charity law in these matters. The document is 112 pages long and not entirely accessible in style or language, but Chapter 1 at least should be read by every member of the PCC. The Church Accounting Regulations 1997–2001 are appended to the document. These provide for compliance with the Charity Commission's

Statement of Recommended Practice 2000 (SORP 2000) but will need to be amended to comply with SORP 2005, which PCCs preparing accruals accounts should use for the accounting period beginning on 1 January 2006. (SORP 2005 can be downloaded from the Charity Commission's website at <http://www.charity-commission.gov.uk/investigations/sorp/sorp05docs.asp>.) *The Charities Act 1993 and the PCC* explains the need for compliance:

> The law makes it clear that charities are accountable to the public for the resources they control. The Charity accounting regulations seek to provide a regime in which charitable organizations receiving funds for public benefit are able to demonstrate to the public that they have observed the trust placed in them in handling and use of those funds. Previously, accountability of charities was largely on the basis of trust; the Regulations additionally require that charities' activities are fully disclosed to the public. PCCs too must demonstrate accountability, though in many cases this will be primarily to a narrower section of the public. Any misuse of funds by PCCs is a matter of general concern.[20]

Annual report

One of the first steps in making PCCs accountable has involved the production, in addition to the annual accounts, of an annual report on the way in which the PCC has discharged its responsibilities. The Charity Commission defines an annual report as 'a concise but comprehensive review of the activities of the charity prepared by the trustees for each accounting year'.[21] This is to be presented to the Annual Parochial Church Meeting (APCM) in accordance with the requirements of the Church Representation Rules. Rather than looking on this as a chore, PCCs should see the annual report and accounts as a tool. The report on the proceedings of the PCC and general activities of the parish enables the wider parish to see how the PCC stewards its resources and conducts its affairs. It can be used to publicize parish activities, to record achievements and to highlight needs.

SORP 2005 lists the following as the required content of the trustees' annual report:

1 Reference and administrative details of the charity, its trustees and advisers.
2 Structure, governance and management.
3 Objectives and activities.
4 Achievements and performance.

5 Financial review.
6 Plans for future periods.
7 Funds held as custodian trustee on behalf of others.

These requirements can be met in this way:

1 A PCC is, as we have already noted a number of times, an *excepted* charity but the majority of the requirements, though modified by the Church Accounting Regulations, apply to the PCC. The annual report, therefore, must give the name and address of the church, list any staff, and give the names and addresses of the inspecting architect, the bankers and auditors. It must also list the members of the Parochial Church Council. The Church Representation Rules [CRRs 16(1)] specify that members are to be elected for a three-year period (unless the Annual Meeting specifically takes a decision that they should hold office for one year only [see CRRs 16(3)]), and it is helpful to indicate the date on which the term of office ends.
2 The annual report will need to record the constitution of the PCC (under the Parochial Church Councils (Powers) Measure 1956) as a body corporate, how members are ex officio, elected or co-opted, how they are inducted and trained, and the relationship between the PCC and the diocesan authorities. This section should conclude with a statement that risk assessment has been carried out and appropriate procedures are in place. (It does not need to list the risks considered.)
3 The third section requires the PCC to set down the aims and objectives of the organization, around the primary objective of 'co-operation with the minister in promoting in the parish the whole mission of the Church, pastoral, evangelistic, social and ecumenical'.
4 The fourth section requires a description of performance and achievements in quantitative (electoral roll numbers, communicants, baptisms, etc.) and qualitative terms. Graphs can be useful to help people readily understand statistics. The statistical section may then be followed by a review of the year, highlighting major events and particular achievements or challenges, and recording thanks to individuals and organizations. The annual report will also state how many times the PCC met during the year and list the main items of business that it discussed.
5 The annual report must include a description of financial activities, including the performance of stewardship and Gift Aid

schemes, in support of the PCC's objectives, together with a statement about reserves and investment policies, as appropriate.

6 The annual report also needs to look forward to what the PCC plans to do – e.g. educational, missionary and evangelistic endeavours, fabric works, etc. – and why – e.g. to be in compliance with the Diocesan Mission Statement.

7 This is not usually relevant to PCCs.

The scene is then set for financial information to be presented in accordance with the appropriate provisions governing annual reports and accounts.[22]

Annual financial statements

All PCCs with a gross income of more than £100,000 a year must prepare accounts using the accruals basis, incorporating a Statement of Financial Activities (SOFA), providing analysis of all incoming resources and the application of those resources, together with a balance sheet and explanatory notes. (The term 'accruals basis' refers to an accounting convention in which transactions are reflected in the accounts of the period in which they take place, as opposed to the period in which payments are made or received.)

SORP 2005 describes the balance sheet as providing 'a snapshot of the charity's assets and liabilities at the end of its accounting year and how assets are split between the different types of funds'. The objective is 'to show the resources available to the charity and whether these are freely available or have to be used for specific purposes because of legal restrictions on their use'.[23] Where applicable, details must be given of funds held by the PCC with specific legal restrictions (e.g. a fund to maintain a tomb or mausoleum, or to provide 'exotic flowers for Easter').

PCCs whose annual gross income is less than £100,000 may prepare their accounts on a receipts and payments (R&P), rather than an accruals, basis (unless they elect to have their accounts scrutinized by a registered auditor – see below).

In the case of teams, united benefices and pluralities, the principle to be borne in mind is that the legal entity is the PCC, and so it is the PCC which must prepare the accounts for the ecclesiastical parish. Accordingly, each parish within a united benefice or plurality must produce accounts in the statutory format, and teams which consist of a number of separate parishes must produce accounts at the level of each parish. In the case of different congregations organized as a team within a single parish, accounts that meet the statutory requirements must be prepared for the parish as a whole. Even where teams comprise a single parish in which there are highly developed District Church Councils (DCCs), accounts meeting the statutory requirements must be produced at PCC, not DCC, level. *The Charities Act 1993 and the PCC* makes this position quite clear when it states:

> While certain responsibilities can be passed down from the PCC to DCCs, this is not the case with financial responsibility which must by law stay with the PCC. DCCs cannot hold assets, they do not have body corporate status and they should not be taking financial decisions and signing contracts with a financial element. Of course the PCC can decide that DCCs can operate within an agreed budget but the PCC is the only legal entity that is able to enter into a contract.[24]

Risk management

There is also a requirement for larger PCCs (those with a gross annual income of £250,000 or more) to consider the financial risks to which they are exposed and the ways in which they will mitigate those risks, and to include a statement in the annual report confirming that this has been done and that suitable risk management systems are in place. PCCs whose gross annual income is less than £250,000 are not specifically required to do this, but it is strongly recommended in *The Charities Act 1993 and the PCC* that they should nevertheless make such a statement.

The Charity Commission identifies five areas of risk for charities:

- Governance risks – e.g. inappropriate organizational structure, difficulties recruiting trustees with relevant skills, conflicts of interest.
- Operational risks – e.g. service quality and development, contract pricing, employment issues, health and safety issues, fraud and misappropriation.
- Financial risks – e.g. accuracy and timeliness of financial information, adequacy of reserves and cash flow, diversity of income sources, investment management.
- External risks – e.g. public perception and adverse publicity, demographic changes, government policy.
- Compliance with law and regulation – e.g. breach of trust law, employment law, and regulative requirements of particular activities such as fund-raising or the running of care facilities.[25]

Likelihood of occurrence (chance of happening)	III High likelihood Low severity of impact	IV High likelihood High severity of impact
	I Low likelihood Low severity of impact	II Low likelihood High severity of impact
	Level of severity of impact on the charity	

Figure 3.1 Assessed risk chart

Risk assessment does not require esoteric formulae; it needs:

- transparency – we should not wittingly or unwittingly conceal risk;
- experience – seeking advice on risk when there is doubt about it;
- assumptions to be checked and clearly presented;
- discipline – so that risk is not taken on without planning; and above all
- common sense.

The basic method of risk assessment asks five questions:

1 What are the risks?
2 How significant are they?
3 What can we do about them?
4 What will we do about them?
5 How are we getting on?

When a risk is identified, it needs to be put into perspective in terms of how likely it is to happen and the impact on the charity if it did happen. Risks ranked as both high in likelihood and high in impact clearly need more immediate attention than those low in both categories. Once identified and assessed, risks can be placed on a chart (see Figure 3.1 above) so that trustees can determine what action, if any, is necessary.

Providing copies of the accounts

In addition to being presented to the APCM, the financial statements of the PCC must also be displayed on the church notice-board for at least seven days – to include at least one Sunday – before the annual meeting. Within 28 days of the annual meeting, a copy must be sent to the secretary of the diocesan board of finance.

In addition, in order to comply with charity legislation, the PCC must provide copies of their accounts, upon written request, to members of the public. The Charity Commission states that all charities must:

> make the accounts available to the public on request. This is vital underpinning to the principle of public accountability, and must be complied with in all cases. It is open to trustees to make a reasonable charge to cover the costs of complying with the request (e.g. photocopying and postage). As a matter of good practice we recommend that a copy of the charity's Annual Report should, wherever possible, be sent with the accounts.[26]

The annual financial statements, as well as the accounting records which are maintained on a day-to-day basis (from which the required accounts will be prepared and which must be sufficient to show and explain all the PCC's transactions), must be preserved for at least six years from the end of the financial year to which they relate.

Can there be a simplified version of the church accounts?

Many people find the format of the church annual accounts confusing. They are intended to give a picture of activity during the year and the financial position on 31 December of the previous year. They must accord with the accounting regulations laid down by the Archbishops' Council to ensure that PCCs, as excepted charities, provide a Statement of Financial Activities that satisfies the requirements of the Charity Commission's Statement of Recommended Practice. The PCC has to agree the annual report and accounts in this form. They are the PCC's accounts and are 'received' by the APCM. Although it will involve more work for the treasurer, the accounts can also be presented to the APCM in simpler form. The PCC should, anyway, have management accounts (i.e. accounts that enable them to make responsible financial decisions) available to them during the year.

To arrange for independent examination or audit of the financial statements

PCCs whose annual gross income is in excess of £250,000 must arrange for their accounts to have a statutory audit by a registered auditor. (The Charities Bill currently before Parliament, however, proposes

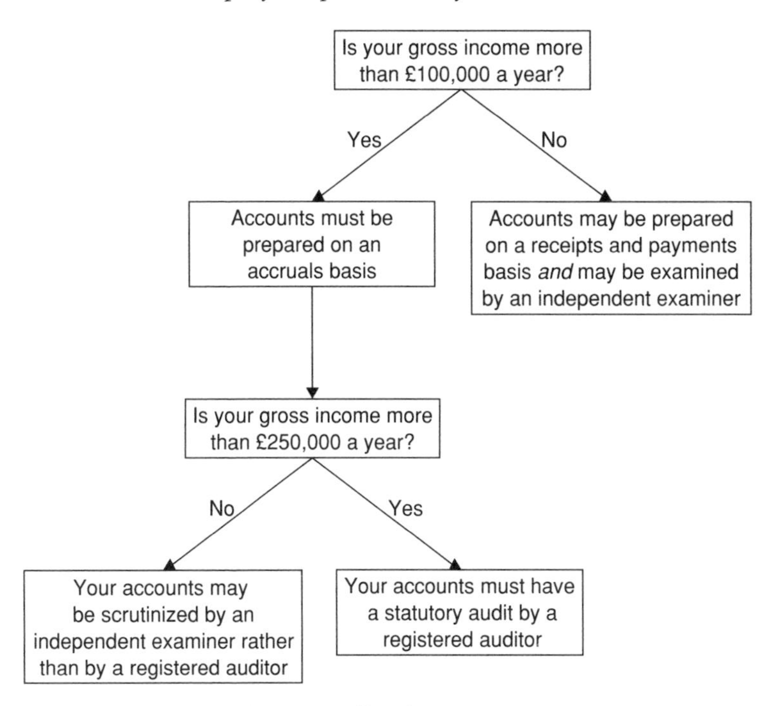

Figure 3.2 Examination or audit of accounts

that an audit requirement should apply only to charities with income over £500,000 or total assets of more than £2.8 million.)

PCCs whose annual gross income is less than £250,000 may if they wish have their accounts scrutinized by an independent examiner, rather than by a registered auditor.

If PCCs whose annual gross income is less than £100,000 elect to have their accounts scrutinized by a registered auditor (this may sometimes be required by the terms of a grant to the PCC) rather than by an independent examiner, they must prepare the accounts on an accruals, rather than an R&P, basis.

Even PCCs whose annual gross income is less than £10,000 are required by the Church Accounting Regulations 1997 to 2001 and the CRRs to have an independent examination of their accounts.

The appointment of an independent examiner or auditor should be made at the APCM. If for some reason it is not made then, or if the person appointed cannot undertake the role, the PCC may appoint someone for a term of office ending at the close of the next APCM. To be 'independent' the examiner must have no connection with the PCC – that is, he or she must not be a member of the PCC, or an employee of the PCC, or related to a member or employer. He or she can, however, be a member of the congregation and on the electoral roll. The independent examiner or auditor may be remunerated.

Professional fees

Larger PCCs will often need to pay professional fees and charges to auditors, solicitors, insurers and other professional advisers. These may well rise year on year and, from time to time, perhaps every five years, the officers of the PCC should see whether the same service can be obtained at a lower cost. In the case of the auditors, for example, the treasurer can write to say that, prior to the appointment being made at the next APCM, he or she will be seeking a tender from a number of accountancy firms.

Once a long-list of possible firms has been compiled, a tender document should be prepared setting out the legal requirement for audit. It should include:

- a statement on the governance of the parish;
- the last two years' audited accounts;
- an indication of the sort of auditor required (e.g. previous church experience, particular expertise, attendance at PCC and/or APCM);
- a timetable of the audit year including when draft accounts will be available and the date when they will be needed for approval by the PCC and presentation to the APCM;
- an indication of how often auditing services will be reviewed by tender.

It should also explain the process and timetable for the appointment of the auditor.

The firms tendering for the audit should be asked to provide information about:

- details of the firm and its capabilities;
- relevant clients;
- audit philosophy and method;
- references that can be taken up;
- the partner and staff who will be assigned to the audit and how continuity will be assured;
- the approach to and timetable for the audit;
- proposed fees for the next three years both for the audit and for any additional work, plus the basis for charging expenses, the

billing schedule and the way in which fees will be set and agreed in future years.

A sub-committee of the PCC should examine the tenders, scoring each firm against the criteria. The preferred two or three should normally be asked to meet the sub-committee, and an appointment can be made thereafter. A letter should set out the terms of the appointment.

To care for and maintain the churchyard

Another area of responsibility specified in the fourth clause of the Parochial Church Councils (Powers) Measure 1921 concerned 'The care and maintenance of the churchyard (including a closed churchyard) with all rights now possessed by the Churchwardens to recover from the overseers the cost of maintaining a closed churchyard'. Responsibility for the churchyard, whether or not it is open for burials, includes maintenance, in terms of grass-cutting etc., and concern for the safety of tombstones and monuments. There may also be contracts with the local authority. A useful document entitled *Responsible Care for Churchyards: A brief practical guide for parishes* can be found at <http://www.cofe.anglican.org/about/churchcommissioners/pastoral/churchproperty/careofchurchyards.doc>.

To consult with the incumbent on matters of general concern and importance to the parish

The Parochial Church Council (Powers) Measure 1921 (repeated in 1956) stated under the heading 'General functions of council' that: 'It shall be the duty of the minister and the parochial church council to consult together on matters of general concern and importance to the parish'. This sounds like a very open-ended duty, along the lines of 'how long is a piece of string?' As if that were not enough, the 1956 Measure broadened this function to embrace 'the consideration and discussion of matters concerning the Church of England or any other matters of religious or public interest, but not the declaration of doctrine of the Church on any question'. In relation to this function the PCC is to be seen as the provider of 'grassroots' opinion to be conveyed upwards through its representation on deanery and thence to diocesan synods, and beyond to General Synod. Sometimes specific questions may come down from one of these bodies to be discussed at PCC level. The Measure goes on to list these specific functions:

- Making known and putting into effect any provision made by the diocesan synod or the deanery synod, but without prejudice to the powers of the council on any particular matter;
- Giving advice to the diocesan synod and the deanery synod on any matter referred to the council;
- Raising such matters as the council consider appropriate with the diocesan synod or deanery synod.

To co-operate with the incumbent in promoting the mission of the Church

The Parochial Church Councils (Powers) Measure 1921 stated, in its second clause: 'It shall be the primary duty of the Council in every parish to co-operate with the Incumbent in the initiation, conduct and development of Church work both within the parish and outside.' This statement apparently owed its origin to Dr Watts-Ditchfield, the first Bishop of Chelmsford.[27] It does not imply that the PCC is subordinate to the incumbent, but rather asserts the duty of the council to take part in the spiritual work of the parish and not to limit its concerns to finance and property. This responsibility was further defined in the Parochial Church Councils (Powers) Measure 1956 as 'co-operation with the minister in promoting in the parish the whole mission of the Church, pastoral, evangelistic, social and ecumenical'. We have already discussed aspects of this primary duty in Chapter 1.

The PCC as employer

Among the powers specified in the seventh clause of the Parochial Church Councils (Powers) Measure 1956 is:

> jointly with the minister to appoint and dismiss the parish clerk and sexton or any persons performing or assisting to perform the duties of parish clerk or sexton and to determine their salaries and the conditions of the tenure of their offices or of their employment but subject to the rights of any persons holding the said offices at the appointed day.

The employees of the PCC fall into five categories:

1. Lay workers, as defined by Canon E 7, who are admitted and licensed under Canon E 8. Though paid by the PCC, a lay worker serves 'under the direction of the minister', in terms specified by the bishop's licence.

2 Those who perform some of the duties traditionally associated with the office of parish clerk, e.g. administrators of various sorts.
3 Those who perform some of the duties traditionally associated with the office of sexton, e.g. maintenance, gardening, vergers' duties, etc.
4 Organists.
5 Those who discharge the offices of the PCC – e.g. treasurer, secretary or electoral roll officer – *and* are paid to do so.

As the employer of paid staff working for a church, the PCC carries the same legal responsibilities as any other employer.

It is essential whenever a PCC is acting as an employer that it fully understands its responsibilities, that employment legislation is adhered to (the Employment Rights Act 1996 is the key piece of legislation here), and that the financial arrangements are clear and robust. Help and advice are available from ACAS, and a useful publication is *The Good Employment Guide for the Voluntary Sector*, published by the National Council for Voluntary Organisations (NCVO). PCCs are rarely used to being employers and might be well advised to seek legal advice before employing anyone for the first time.

A helpful working definition of 'employee' in a parochial context can be found in a report produced by the diocese of Blackburn in December 2000 entitled *Employment of Lay Workers: Guidelines for Parishes* and available at the diocese's website <http://www.blackburn.anglican.org/index.htm>: 'an individual who works in a parish and receives some form of remuneration from the parish (either honorarium, hourly wage or salary) and who is employed by the PCC'. The type of posts for which the PCC might be the employer range from full-time administrator to part-time gardener, and could include cleaners, organists, vergers, youth workers, fund-raisers, project managers and caretakers.

Recruitment

The first aspect to consider is the recruitment process. Prior to advertising a post the PCC should ideally have drawn up and agreed an equal opportunities policy. A form of words could be as follows:

> Recruitment, selection, training, and consideration for promotion for those who work within our organization are available to all without unfair discrimination, and we will work to ensure that no one is disadvantaged in any of these matters by conditions and requirements that cannot be shown to be justifiable. We will work to ensure that there is no discrimination on the grounds of race, colour, nationality (including

citizenship), ethnic or national origins, disability, age, gender, married or single status, where any of these cannot be shown to be a requirement of the job and office concerned.

If the person appointed will be required to go through the Criminal Records Bureau (CRB) Disclosure process, this needs to be stated in any advertisement or other recruitment literature.

Prior to recruitment the PCC also needs to have drawn up and agreed a job description for the post. A clear job description can prevent all kinds of difficulties arising in the future, such as misunderstandings about who does what, who reports to whom, where one person's job ends and another's begins. A job description is also an essential tool for management, in reviewing an employee's work, assessing training needs and deciding whether a role needs to be developed. Alongside the job description there should be a person specification, describing the kind of experience, qualifications, talents and personal qualities likely to be present in the ideal candidate for the job. Job description and person specification should naturally fit together. The job description should state if there is to be a probationary period and how long it will be. The PCC should decide how many referees will be required, what categories they might fall into (present employer, a priest, etc.), and whether references should be requested from the candidate at the time of application or at the time of shortlisting or be requested by the PCC prior to or after interview. This will determine the interview and appointment timescale (i.e. more time must be allowed before interview if references must be received by then).

The advertisement – in the *Church Times*, *Church of England Newspaper* or other appropriate publication – should briefly indicate the nature of the position, remuneration, accommodation (if provided), closing date for applications, date for interview, date for commencement, and the way in which further information can be obtained (website or other address; a telephone number or e-mail address encourages enquiry by those means). The material sent to enquirers should give the timetable in full: applications by, shortlisting on, interviews on, start date. Those responsible for the interview process must stick to this timetable and notify people promptly if they have not been shortlisted or appointed. The PCC should agree on the make-up of the shortlisting and interview panels and consider whether there should be an outside interviewer (e.g. someone from the diocese, someone with HR (Human Resources) skills).

The selection process is not easy and can be full of pitfalls. The shortlisting panel should carefully read all the applications and check them against the criteria for appointment. Those who clearly don't fit at all should be notified that they have not been shortlisted. A shortlist of between three and six candidates should be agreed, depending on the strength of the field. A programme for the day or half-day should be drawn up, offering candidates a chance to see the church, school, parish plant and facilities, accommodation, etc., as appropriate, depending on the position being filled. The order of interviewing may depend on travel times, otherwise it can be determined by drawing names out of a hat. The interview panel should agree a list of questions and put them to each of the shortlisted candidates, endeavouring to find the closest match between the individuals interviewed and the person specification. If the person needs to have certain skills (e.g. computer skills or, in the case of a musician, organ and conducting skills), there should be an opportunity for these to be tested or demonstrated. Do not be afraid not to appoint if no one comes near the requirements of the person specification. It is better to have an unfilled post than an employment disaster. And if you do appoint someone (after taking up references), and they seem perfect in every respect, still make sure that you have a probationary period in place and that you stick with it.

More often in the church than in other organizations, someone just emerges to fill a job, often from the congregation, without advertisement or formal interview procedure. In these cases you should still ensure a properly agreed job description and remuneration package are drawn up and implemented, and have a CV and references on file.

As mentioned above, certain posts carry with them the necessity of CRB Disclosure before the new employee can be confirmed in post. These include posts of people who will be working with children (compulsory) and posts requiring handling of money (advisable). Standard Disclosure is primarily for positions that involve working with children or regular contact with vulnerable adults. It contains details of all convictions on record (including spent convictions) and details of any cautions, reprimands or warnings. For positions involving working with children, Standard Disclosure will also give any information contained in government department lists of people considered unsuitable to work with children. Enhanced Disclosure is applicable to positions that involve regularly caring for, training, supervising, or being in sole charge of children or vulnerable adults.

It involves an extra level of checking with local police records in addition to checks with the Police National Computer and government department lists, where appropriate. Individual diocesan authorities will have systems in place for how the disclosure is managed, but further information can be obtained from the Criminal Records Bureau website at <http://www.crb.gov.uk>.

Contracts of employment

In addition to the job description and person specification, a contract of employment needs to be drawn up; this will be signed by the employee and by somebody on behalf of the PCC (probably the incumbent as chairman) once the appointment has been made. (It is important to be aware that a contract of service exists once an employer and employee have agreed upon the terms and conditions of the employment, even if the agreement is not in writing.) The contract should specify the terms and conditions of employment, including the rate of pay (which must, of course, be at least equal to the national minimum wage), holiday entitlement (specifying if it has to be taken at certain times, e.g. Holy Week), and overtime arrangements, if any. Other terms and conditions which should be covered in the contract include the circumstances in which deductions may be made from wages (there are very limited circumstances in which this may happen, such as when a loan has been made to an employee by an employer and repayments are deducted from wages), time off work for public duties and other matters, suspension from work on health and safety grounds, arrangements for sick pay, maternity and paternity rights, termination of employment, grounds for dismissal, and redundancy. You should have a clear policy on the payment of legitimate expenses associated with the post and a means of accounting for them. You also need agreed procedures for induction, grievances and discipline.

If you are employing someone for the first time, you will also have to get to grips with deducting tax and National Insurance contributions from their pay, as well as making the employer's contribution to National Insurance. Information is available from your local HM Revenue and Customs office, from the New Employer Helpline (NESI) (Tel: 0845 60 70 143) and from HM Revenue and Customs' website at <http://www.hmrc.gov.uk/employers/index.shtml>. Information on pensions is available from the Pension Service at <http://www.thepensionservice.gov.uk>.

Job descriptions should be reviewed on a regular basis, at least once a year, and amendments should be made in the light of experience, changing circumstances, and the particular strengths and weaknesses of the employee. The review and the revised job description that emerges from it should be used to enable the employer and the employee to meet the developing needs of the organization (in this case, the church) and of one another, and you should not feel that the description is set in stone. Job descriptions should not be allowed to gather dust in a filing cabinet; they are tools to be used by employer and employee alike.

In addition to the contract of employment, it may be useful for the main rules of the organization to be provided in written form to all employees. These may take the form of a 'code of conduct'. The NCVO advises that the rules should be stated clearly in order to avoid any misunderstandings, and that special care should be taken to ensure all employees entering the working environment for the first time understand them. The rules, or code of conduct, may include examples of the sort of behaviour which would constitute gross misconduct and therefore lead to summary dismissal.

Employment legislation

The Employment Rights Act 1996 requires employers to provide their employees with details of what to do in the event of having a grievance, including specifying the person whom employees should approach. In addition, as a matter of good practice, it is recommended that a grievance policy be drawn up, adopted by the PCC and given to the employee. A grievance policy should state that employees must be given a fair hearing concerning any grievance they may have, and that they have a right to be accompanied by a colleague or trade union official when raising a grievance.

The kinds of issues concerning which an employee may feel he or she has a grievance which affects their well-being and thus their ability to carry out their work effectively include harassment, intimidation, bullying, incompetent colleagues, a dangerous work environment, a lack of resources to do the job properly, or too great a workload. To address these matters before they arise, the PCC may wish to draw up specific grievance policies covering particular areas of concern, such as sexual harassment or bullying. Such policies should clearly define the type of behaviour prohibited by them and spell out the disciplinary consequences of indulging in such behaviour.

It is important that employers take grievances and complaints seriously. If they are not addressed properly, an employee may feel he or she is unable to go on working for you. If they have been employed by you for more than a year they could, on resignation, make a claim for constructive dismissal as a result of the employer's inaction. (Any claim for constructive dismissal must be brought within three months of the employee's resignation.) Complaints of unfair dismissal or discrimination, or various other employment matters such as breach of contract, can, unless resolved by the parties involved, be heard by Employment Tribunals, which may order reinstatement or compensation. The right to a hearing on a complaint of unfair dismissal applies only to workers who have been employed for more than 12 months. (Should your PCC be unfortunate enough to become embroiled in a dispute of this sort, do remember to check the PCC's insurance policy as you may find it provides cover for at least some of the costs involved.)

Other legislation affecting employers and employees includes the Equal Pay Act 1970, the Rehabilitation of Offenders Act 1974, the Children Act 1989 (sometimes referred to – erroneously – as the Child Protection Act 1989), the Sex Discrimination Act 1975, the Race Relations Act 1976, the Employment Equality Regulations 2003, the Health and Safety at Work Act 1974, the Management of Health and Safety at Work Regulations 1999, the Disability Discrimination Acts 1995 and 2005, the Working Time Regulations 1998, the Data Protection Act 1998, the Fire Precautions (Workplace) Regulations 1997 and the Regulatory Reform (Fire Safety) Order 2005.

The Equal Pay Act 1970

This requires employers to pay men and women an equal wage when the work they do is of equal value.

The Rehabilitation of Offenders Act 1974

This states that job applicants do not have to reveal that they are former offenders if they have been sentenced to no more than 30 months' imprisonment and have served a period of rehabilitation. For certain jobs, however – particularly for those which include work with young people under the age of 18 – there is no rehabilitation period and past convictions must be declared.

The Children Act 1989

The House of Bishops has stated that the Church of England accepts the principle enshrined in the Children Act 1989 that the welfare of the child is paramount. A PCC policy on child protection, though tailored to the needs of the local parish, must be based on the recommendations of the House of Bishops' revised policy on child protection[28] and any guidelines issued by the diocese (each diocese may have its own variations), as well as meeting the requirements stated under the Act and the Home Office's guidelines. The House of Bishops' publication *Protecting All God's Children*, which contains the third edition of the House of Bishops' policy on child protection, includes a series of procedures to be followed in carrying out safe recruitment of those working with children. The PCC must also ensure that it has adequate insurance cover, including public liability insurance, for all activities organized by the church and held at the church that involve children. (The Children Act 1989 defines a child as a person under 18 for most purposes.)

The Sex Discrimination Act 1975

This is concerned with both direct and indirect discrimination. Direct discrimination is when an employee has been treated less favourably than another in similar circumstances on the grounds of gender. Indirect discrimination occurs when a requirement is applied equally to male and female employees, but one gender is unable to comply. The most common example of indirect discrimination is a requirement for full-time working, which generally fewer women than men can do by reason of their child-care commitments. In these circumstances, the test tends to be whether the employer can justify their requirement for full-time work.

The Race Relations Act 1976

This is also concerned with both direct and indirect discrimination.

The Employment Equality Regulations 2003

The Employment Equality (Sexual Orientation) Regulations 2003 and the Employment Equality (Religion or Belief) Regulations 2003 outlaw discrimination in employment or vocational training on the grounds of sexual orientation and religion or belief, and are therefore of particular concern to church and other Christian organizations. The Archbishops' Council has produced a paper on the implementation of these regulations; the Gloucester diocesan website usefully reproduces it at <http://www.glosdioc.org.uk/Home/EmpEq.pdf>. Both sets of regulations do allow for exceptions in the case of a 'genuine occupational requirement' (GOR), but the Archbishops' Council points out that a blanket policy of requiring all workers to be Christians or Anglicans will no longer be sustainable under these regulations which 'require an employer to show that affiliations of religion or belief are proportionate in relation to the particular post in question'. These regulations are not something to be frightened of but to be aware of when drawing up job descriptions and recruitment advertisements, which should 'clearly but sensitively state the position of the place of worship, parish or diocese on any requirement it imposes'. The Archbishops' Council makes the point, for instance, that 'some PCCs may conclude that it is proportionate to insist that a Christian should fill a particular secretarial or administrative post because it includes a local representational role for the Church with substantial contact with the public and a pastoral dimension'. A sexual-orientation GOR is bound to be harder (though not necessarily impossible) to justify than a religion or belief one.

The Health and Safety at Work Act 1974 (and The Management of Health and Safety at Work Regulations 1999)

These require employers to provide and maintain a safe working environment and safe systems at work. It also requires them to ensure that non-employees, such as visitors, are not endangered by work activities, and that employees are trained in how to ensure a safe working environment. As the Ecclesiastical Insurance Group (EIG, see <http://www.ecclesiastical.co.uk>) points out, churches present a vast range of health and safety issues, from food handling to working at high levels (or to the trip hazards of an uneven floor). Local authority environmental health officers are responsible for enforcing health and safety legislation in churches, as elsewhere. They have the power to enter a church at any time to ensure that you are complying with the law.

The law states that where you have five or more employees you must have a written health and safety policy, but it still makes sense to have one even if you have fewer than five employees. EIG is willing to make available to all parishes, free of charge, a detailed draft health and safety policy. It can be obtained by attending a seminar run by an Ecclesiastical Insurance consultant and surveyor. The seminars last about an hour and are specifically designed to help you get to grips with health and safety issues.

EIG suggests that PCCs appoint a particular individual to take overall responsibility for health and safety, and possibly set up a sub-committee or working party of the PCC to deal with these issues. EIG also offers a round-the-clock advice line if you have any enquiries regarding health and safety or employment law. The number is 0117 934 2104.

The Disability Discrimination Act 1995

This applies only to those who employ 15 or more people. It could nevertheless reasonably be considered good practice for the church to make an effort to recruit disabled workers and to make reasonable provision for them to be able to do their work.

The Working Time Regulations 1998

This places a statutory limit on working hours for most employees. It also requires employers to provide paid holidays, breaks and minimum rest periods.

The Data Protection Act 1998

Employers are data processors for the purposes of the Data Protection Act and accordingly must ensure that personal data about employees is obtained and retained only for specific and lawful purposes.

Employees have the right to request copies of data that is held about them, and to receive a copy of their personnel file, excluding confidential references about them given by their previous employer. A charge of up to £10 may be levied by the employer. Any inaccuracies in data should be remedied as soon as possible.

The Fire Precautions (Workplace) Regulations 1997

When the church building is also a workplace (e.g. the parish office is located in the building or you have a verger or bookstall attendant working in the church), you need to comply with these regulations which include the following provisions: '(a) a workplace shall, to the extent that is appropriate, be equipped with appropriate fire-fighting equipment and with fire detectors and alarms; and (b) any non-automatic fire-fighting equipment so provided shall be easily accessible, simple to use and indicated by signs.' One or more employees will need to be given responsibility for fire-fighting and for training other employees. Churches which are also workplaces are subject to inspection by the local fire brigade to ensure that the regulations are being complied with; in the case of non-compliance, the fire brigade can serve an enforcement notice. Even if the church is not used as a workplace, it does of course make good sense to have fire extinguishers in place, fire exits clearly marked and sidesmen trained in fire-fighting and evacuation procedures.

The Regulatory Reform (Fire Safety) Order 2005

This came into effect on 1 April 2006 and relates to all non-domestic premises. The PCC is responsible for complying with this order, as are also building, maintenance and safety contractors when they are working on the premises. The main duties under the order are to:

- carry out a risk assessment;
- consider those at risk;
- take preventative and protective action;
- prepare a personal emergency evacuation plan (PEEP);
- carry out training of those responsible (e.g. sidesmen) in the use of fire-fighting equipment (fire extinguishers) and evacuation procedures;
- review the risk assessment annually.

(See full text of the order at <http://www.opsi.gov.uk/si/si2005/20051541.htm>.)

An employment checklist

(adapted from that provided in the Diocese of Blackburn's document, *Employment of Lay Workers: Guidelines for Parishes*)

- What wage/salary do you propose to pay, and will it be uprated annually?
- Is there a job description and has this been agreed by the PCC?
- Are you sure that the rate of pay you propose conforms to the national minimum wage (from 1 October 2006, this is £5.35 an hour for

persons aged 22 and over; £4.45 for those aged 18 to 21; and £3.30 for 16- and 17-year-olds)?

- Have you prepared a contract which specifies terms and conditions – e.g. holidays, overtime?
- Have you a clear policy on the payment of legitimate expenses associated with the post?
- Are there agreed procedures for induction, grievance and discipline?
- Have you taken into account the need for the employer's contribution to National Insurance? (currently required for pay above £84 per week).
- Do you know how to deal with income tax? (Information available from your local HM Revenue and Customs office, or from <http://www.hmrc.gov.uk.>)
- Has the PCC defined its policies on equal opportunities, health and safety, and child protection?

The use of volunteers

Many PCCs are more likely to be working with volunteers than with employees, but there are issues to take note of here too. In particular, care needs to be taken to avoid volunteers inadvertently being treated as employees, thus laying the way open for a disgruntled ex-volunteer to make a claim with the Employment Tribunals for unfair dismissal. A particularly useful resource on both employment and volunteer issues is 'askNCVO', an online best-practice resource for the voluntary sector, maintained by the National Council for Voluntary Organisations (NCVO) and accessible from their website at <http://www.ncvo-vol.org.uk/>.

There is currently no legislation specifically covering volunteer workers, nor is there any legal definition of who constitutes a volunteer worker. There are certain things you should be careful of in order to ensure volunteers do not become employees in the eyes of the law. For instance, though volunteers may welcome – and indeed require – training, any agreement you have with a volunteer should not characterize training as a right. Instead, the agreement can express the intention of training being offered when and where possible in order to help the volunteer carry out his or her particular role effectively. Training should be given only when it can be seen to be directly related to the work the volunteer is doing. Furthermore, an organization is not entitled to require anything from its volunteers, such as a minimum time commitment, in return for training. Binding arrangements of this sort have been ruled by the courts to constitute a contract of employment.

Though it is safer to avoid 'contracts' for volunteers, which can lead to false expectations of obligation on both sides, it is nevertheless good practice to have a written agreement. This can include a role description (note not 'job' description) and it can help both parties to clarify their intentions and expectations. In order to avoid an 'agreement' becoming a 'contract', it is important not to write about, or imply, the existence of rights and obligations. Instead you should concentrate on such concepts as intentions, hopes or policies, thus reflecting the voluntary nature of the arrangement. Likewise, though it is good practice to reimburse volunteers for expenses they have incurred while working for you, the safest option is to reimburse only actual expenses, preferably against receipts. To pay an 'expenses' per diem, automatically, can be seen in tribunals as the equivalent of paying a salary (albeit a very small one). Examples of legitimate expenses which may be paid to volunteers include:

- travel to and from the place of volunteering;
- travel undertaken in the course of volunteering;
- meals taken during the course of volunteering;
- postage and telephone costs if the volunteer is working from home;
- protective clothing or other essential equipment;
- child-care expenses.

Despite the necessity of ensuring volunteers do not accidentally become employees, there are certain aspects of employment and other legislation which necessarily cover volunteers too. Chief among these is the requirement of all volunteers who will be working with children or vulnerable adults to go through the CRB Disclosure process, just like any employee working in those areas. Volunteers also need to be fully covered by appropriate insurance; they, just like paid staff, may face risks of personal injury, liability for accidents, and loss of or damage to property. An organization will also be liable for the negligent actions of its volunteers (such as the provision of incorrect advice or allowing visitors into dangerous parts of a building) and needs to ensure that the public is protected. Ecclesiastical Insurance reports that the Health and Safety Executive is increasingly viewing volunteers as employees and expects them to be provided with the same level of protection.

The NCVO provides the following checklist covering all aspects of volunteer management:

1 Write a volunteering strategy.
2 Write volunteering policies.
3 Write a role description and role specification for each volunteer vacancy.
4 Ensure you have relevant references and CRB checks for each volunteer.
5 Induct all new volunteers and those taking on a new or increased role.
6 Provide training relevant to the volunteer's work or role.
7 Provide highly supportive supervision and management.
8 Ensure volunteer documents do not set out 'rights' or 'obligations'.

You may well feel that it is depressing even to have to consider some of these issues, that in a community based on the love of God, there is no place for grievance, complaint, tribunals, dismissals and allegations. You want to believe that church volunteers are always upright, well-intentioned, and never neurotic people, and that someone applying to work in a church is equally blameless and selfless and would never dream of taking you to an employment tribunal. You would, however, be naive to think so – as any experience of working with the imperfect human beings we all are will surely tell you – and you would be seriously misguided to act on this naive belief and neglect to put all the correct policies in place. Forewarned is forearmed, and it is far better to take time over policies for grievance and discipline which may never have to be implemented than not to do so and find your good intentions have been taken advantage of and you are in a fix. It is also in the best interests of the church as an institution to be shown to be a good employer, exercising due care and consideration over its employees and volunteers as well as ensuring it is protected from inadequate or malicious workers.

'Making representations' to the bishop

One of the powers specified in the eighth clause of the Parochial Church Councils (Powers) Measure 1921 was that 'to make representations to the Bishop with regard to any matter affecting the welfare of the Church in the parish'. This was reaffirmed word for word in the Parochial Church Councils (Powers) Measure 1956. Why would the PCC do this? The fundamental reason is to bring to his attention some important matter concerning the parish. Normally this would be done by the minister and churchwardens through the archdeacon, but there might be a circumstance in which the PCC felt that it was not being heard or being taken seriously and so directed its communication to the bishop directly. This should be done by the PCC secretary, after a resolution of the council, and in a form determined by the council.

Example

The churchwardens reported to the PCC that the vicarage was no longer adequate to the needs of the parish. It was simply in the wrong place. They had spoken to the archdeacon, but he had been unsympathetic. The PCC felt that something had to be done, so it was resolved that representations should be made to the bishop, and the PCC secretary was instructed to write to him, the PCC telling the secretary in what terms her letter should be framed.

Property

Property, such as housing for assistant clergy, or church halls, that is acquired by a parish with the consent of the diocese, is vested in the diocesan authority as the custodian trustees. It can be managed by the PCC but diocesan consent is required for any letting, other than a casual hiring, or for disposal. In making any proposal, the PCC should ask:

1. Is it in the best interest of the parish?
2. Have any restrictions in any trust deed been taken into account?
3. Does it comply with charity legislation?
4. Does it comply with the Landlord and Tenant Act?

Areas which are not the responsibility of the PCC

Albert Mitchell, author of *The Enabling Act and the Powers Measure* (Church Book Room Press, 1947), remarked of the powers specified in the Parochial Church Councils (Powers) Measure 1921 that 'It should be noted that the powers conferred are somewhat limited. There is no roving commission to interfere in all the work of the Parish conferred on the Council or, apart from a representation to the bishop, to interfere with the services of the church.'[29] This is an important observation, and it might make the lives of many incumbents easier were PCC members to adopt the motto: 'no roving commission to interfere'.

A particular point which seems to be frequently ignored is that it is the minister alone who is responsible for the performance of divine service. Other than a decision to change the authorized form of worship (e.g. from the Book of Common Prayer to *Common Worship*), the PCC has no responsibility for services.

Although the minister may want to, and perhaps ought to, discuss the style of worship in the parish with the PCC, there are only two or three areas that require such consultation. The Canons of the Church of England authorize a number of forms of service, among them services in the Book of Common Prayer, services approved by the General Synod (e.g. those in *Common Worship*) and services approved by the convocations, archbishops, bishop or other Ordinary. Canon B 3 provides that decisions about the form of service to be used, other than for the occasional offices (e.g. weddings), are to be taken jointly by the minister and the PCC. If there is disagreement and for as long as the disagreement continues, the services in the Book of Common Prayer are to be used (though certain conditions apply if alternative services have been in use for two out of four years previously). Canon B 8 deals with vesture and it allows a wide range of clerical dress for services but states that 'no minister shall change the form of vesture in the church or chapel in which he officiates unless he has ascertained by consultation with the parochial church council that such changes will be acceptable'. The third area that might require consultation concerns Morning and Evening Prayer and the Holy Communion. Canons B 11 and B 14 set down the requirement to have these services; the requirement may be dispensed with on an occasional basis 'as authorized by the minister and the parochial church council acting jointly', or on a regular basis 'as authorized by the bishop on the request of the minister and the parochial church council acting jointly'.

Any version of the Bible may be used with alternative (i.e. not BCP) services, but when services are from the Book of Common Prayer the Authorized Version and the Prayer Book Psalter are to be used, unless the PCC agrees to another version chosen from those set down in an appendix to the Canons.

In the choice of music the minister is required by canon to 'pay due heed' to the advice and assistance of the director of music, organist or choirmaster, but the final responsibility and decision in such matters as choosing chants, hymns, anthems and other settings rest with the minister. It is not the responsibility of the PCC. The bells also fall under the authority of the incumbent.

♦ 4 ♦

The PCC and its members

A parish is a community. It has its own norms, its own particular ways of being a community. Deciding to join the parish involves a decision to live within those particular ways. This does not mean that it is impossible for a community and its ways to change, but it does imply that if someone joins simply in order to change the community, they are acting under false pretences. And if this is true for someone joining the parish community, it is even more significant for those who seek to join the PCC. A parish may be fairly open, trying to provide a welcome for all who want to be disciples of Christ, but it will also have its own ways, often tried and tested, as well as a sense of purpose and mission, no matter how small it may be – a desire to be Christ's Church in this place.

Membership of the PCC is a form of Christian ministry. It could be said that everyone owes the parish three years' service on the PCC. The council needs members who represent the various congregations that worship in the parish church, and it needs to be representative and well-balanced in terms of gender and age. Some, preferably a majority, of the members should live in the parish, if it is a residential area. A candidate for election should be an active believer and a regular worshipper who also participates in other aspects of parish life. He or she should also be a regular contributor to church funds, preferably through planned tax-effective giving (i.e. stewardship). A candidate should recognize that the PCC is a working body that makes decisions, owns them, implements them and takes responsibility for them. He or she must be willing to attend meetings, to read papers in advance, to contribute to discussion and to act in an appropriate corporate way that respects members' corporate responsibility. A candidate should be in general sympathy with the way in which the parish is being led, and no one should stand for PCC in order to use the council as a platform for dissent. (There will always be people whose aim is to get on to the PCC in order to frustrate the incumbent; this is not a good motive!)

There is no generally agreed 'person specification' for membership of a PCC and no one should feel discouraged from standing if they wish to do so. It is worth checking before you stand, however, that you can answer 'yes' to such questions as:

- Do I have a positive attitude towards my church and do I feel able to co-operate with its minister?
- Can I offer the time commitment required? (i.e. Will I be able to attend most PCC meetings? Will I have time to read any preparatory material? Am I able to attend church on a regular basis? Can I spend some time getting to know other members of the PCC and congregation? Am I prepared to join a sub-committee or working group?)
- Am I prepared to participate fully in meetings by joining in the discussion?
- Am I also prepared to be quiet and to listen?

Another question which you may need to ask yourself is: 'Will I be upset if I don't get elected this time?' An election does mean that some people will get more votes than others and vice versa, and it is important – though not always easy – not to feel personally slighted if you fail to be elected. There can be all kinds of reasons why you may not have amassed as many votes as some other people, and frequently those reasons will have nothing to do with you personally. Sometimes PCCs are aware that they lack expertise in a particular area – say, that of buildings management or perhaps of fund-raising – and so existing members may informally be on the lookout for someone with experience in that area and will vote for such a person. Sometimes church people find it very hard not to go on voting in the same people time after time – often out of a misguided sense of pity ('Oh, poor old Mr Jones would be so upset if he wasn't on the PCC any more') – and so it can be hard for new people to break through. Perhaps no one knows you very well yet; or perhaps the people who would have voted for you just didn't turn up to this year's meeting. If you can demonstrate that your failure to get on to the PCC this time round hasn't dented your support for the church and its congregation, and you get involved in other areas of its activity, then you may very well get on to the PCC the next time you stand. (Or you may decide you'd rather be doing other things anyway!)

As you will by now be aware, the PCC has specific responsibilities, but you do not have to be on the PCC in order to play an active and useful role in your church. The PCC need not, and probably should not, include everyone who takes responsibility for an aspect of the life of the parish. A vast range of tasks can be undertaken by committed lay people who are not necessarily members of the PCC – tasks such as visiting the sick, sharing in baptism, confirmation and wedding preparation, running Sunday school or junior church, undertaking youth work, reading lessons, preparing intercessions, serving, sacristy work, flower-arranging, vestment repair, grass-cutting, gutter-clearing, church cleaning, and so on; the list is virtually endless.

Types of PCC membership

The PCC consists of:

1 All clerks in holy orders beneficed in or licensed to the parish.
2 Any deaconess or lay worker licensed to the parish.
3 In a team ministry, all members of the team.
4 The churchwardens.
5 Such licensed readers on the electoral roll as the annual meeting shall determine.
6 All persons on the electoral roll who are members of the deanery or diocesan synods or the General Synod.
7 The elected representatives of the laity.
8 Co-opted members, not exceeding one fifth of the representatives of the laity or two persons, whichever shall be greater, who may be lay or ordained.

The situation is more complicated in parishes where there is more than one place of worship.

Ex officio members

Ex officio members, or those who are members of the PCC because of the office they hold, include:

- All the clergy ('clerks in holy orders') beneficed in or licensed to the parish (but not clergy who simply have permission to officiate in the parish or in the diocese generally, with the exception of any clerk in holy orders who has been authorized to chair the PCC) (see Chapter 5 on officers of the PCC).

- Any deaconess or lay worker licensed to the parish.
- In a team ministry, all the members of the team.
- The churchwardens (and any deputy churchwardens who have been made ex officio members by a scheme agreed by the annual meeting under CRRs Rule 18(4).
- Readers: CRRs Rule 14(1)(e) states that the annual meeting may determine if any readers licensed to the parish or any part of it, and who are on the electoral roll, should be on the PCC and, if so, how many of them. If the APCM decides that there shall be no ex officio reader, or just one to represent a number of readers, then any reader who is eligible to stand for election may do so in the normal way.
- Lay members of any deanery or diocesan synod, or of the General Synod, whose names are on the electoral roll of the parish. (This is a slightly odd rule. A person can be on the roll of two or more parishes, in the same or different dioceses, and so in theory a person may become an ex officio member of one parish's PCC by virtue of being elected as a deanery synod member at the annual meeting of another parish.)

There are some special provisions in CRRs for group ministries, for parishes with more than one place of worship, and for joint PCCs where there are two or more parishes in a single benefice or where two or more benefices are held in plurality.

Deanery Synod members

Lay representatives are elected to deanery synod at the annual meeting for a period of three years, the three-year term beginning on the 1 June following the election. (So if there are no resignations or changes in numbers of members this election will take place only once every three years.) The numbers to be elected from each parish are determined by a resolution of the diocesan synod, and will be calculated according to the number on the church electoral roll.

Elected lay members

The most important and largest category of PCC membership consists of representatives of the laity. They should always form a sizeable majority. CRRs Rule 14(g) states the number which should be elected (see Table 4.1, p. 62).

Table 4.1 Recommended proportion of elected lay members

Number on electoral roll	*Number to be elected*
50	6
100	9
101–200	12
201–300	15
300+	15

These numbers can be altered by a resolution of the APCM, but any alteration will not come into effect until the following APCM. The numbers, if varied, must be divisible by three if lay members are elected for three years, with one third retiring each year. The CRRs in Rule 16(3) still allow for the possibility, by resolution of the APCM, of elected lay members of the PCC holding office for one year at a time and retiring at the conclusion of the next annual meeting after their election, but the normal rule [Rule 16(1)] is for members to be elected for a three-year term, and to be eligible for re-election – unless the APCM, under CRRs Rule 17, has limited membership to a specified number of years of continuous service. The APCM may also determine that after a specified interval a person again becomes eligible to stand. The period must be determined from the date on which the decision is made and cannot be retrospective.

In June 1997 the Bridge Report, representing the conclusions of a review of synodical government undertaken by Lord Bridge of Harwich, was published. One of its recommendations was that election to PCC should be for a three-year term with one third of the elected lay members retiring annually by rotation; it was held that this provided for greater stability and continuity. This recommendation was implemented in January 2004, and represented a change to the arrangement whereby one-year membership was the norm and three-year membership had to be specifically adopted.

It is possible to switch from the three-year to the one-year system by resolution of the annual meeting, but there are certain transitional arrangements. Let us suppose that there are 12 elected members of the PCC. Four will retire in 2007, four in 2008, and four in 2009, but the 2007 annual meeting decides to adopt one-year terms with immediate effect. This does not shorten the terms of those already elected; they will still retire on their due date, but new elections will be for only one year. So, four will be elected for one year in 2007;

eight for one year in 2008; and 12 for one year in 2009. The decision to have a one-year term has to be reviewed at least once every six years, so it must be reviewed, at the latest, at the 2013 annual meeting. If it is renewed, then it must be reviewed again no later than 2019. If it is revoked, all 12 members are elected at once and lots are drawn to decide who stands for one, two or three years, in order to re-establish the three-year pattern. There obviously need to be very good reasons for switching from the three-year to the one-year system or back again.

Elections of lay representatives to the PCC are conducted at the APCM. Those being nominated must:

- be at least 16 years old;
- be an actual communicant;
- have his or her name entered on the electoral roll of the parish and, unless the candidate is under 18 years of age at the time of election, this must have been the case for the preceding six months.

An 'actual communicant' originally meant someone who receives Communion in the parish at least at Christmas, Easter and Whitsun. It is no longer the case that it must be in the parish or on these particular festivals. CRRs Rule 54 now defines 'actual communicant' as:

> a person who has received communion according to the use of the Church of England or of a Church in communion with the Church of England at least three times during the twelve months preceding the date of his election or appointment being a person whose name is on the roll of the parish and is either –
> (a) confirmed or ready and desirous of being confirmed; or
> (b) receiving the Holy Communion in accordance with the provisions of Canon B 15A paragraph 1(b).

This latter reference is to the permission to admit to the Holy Communion 'baptised persons who are communicant members of other Churches which subscribe to the doctrine of the Holy Trinity, and who are in good standing in their own Church' – in other words, the same people who may be entered on the electoral roll of a parish in the third category (see Chapter 5 on electoral roll officer).

A person may be disqualified from being nominated if he or she is disqualified from being a charity trustee (under the terms of the Charities Act 1993), or disqualified from holding office under section 10(6) of the Incumbents (Vacation of Benefices) Measure 1977 (No. 1). This second disqualification is an interesting one; it comes from the part of the Measure that concerns the breakdown of a pastoral relationship. When there is a serious breakdown in the pastoral relationship between an incumbent and the parishioners a request may be made to the bishop, by the incumbent, the archdeacon or a two-thirds majority of the lay members of the PCC, asking for an enquiry. First, the archdeacon is asked to report (unless the archdeacon is the incumbent or the person making the request) and then, if recommended, an enquiry is made by a provincial tribunal. The procedure is set down in the Measure, and only one possible finding of the tribunal concerns us here. If the tribunal finds that there is a serious breakdown to which the conduct of the incumbent has contributed over a substantial period *and* that the conduct of the parishioners over a substantial period has also contributed to it, then the bishop may rebuke such of the parishioners as he thinks fit and

> may, if he thinks fit, disqualify such of them as he thinks fit from being a churchwarden or officer of the parochial church council of the parish in question and of such other parishes in his diocese as he may specify during such period not exceeding five years as he may specify.

Candidates must be nominated and seconded by persons whose names are entered on the electoral roll of the parish, and must indicate their willingness to stand. The nomination can be made in writing before the APCM, or verbally at the meeting. If the number of nominations does not exceed the number of places available, the candidates are declared to have been elected; otherwise there is an election, by show of hands if no one objects, or by using voting papers.

It can happen that too few people stand for election and that there are vacancies on the PCC. These can be filled as 'casual vacancies' by the PCC itself, but the council might want to ask why there are not enough candidates and what can be done to remedy the situation. This can be achieved by asking a few possible candidates why they didn't stand – the answers might be 'No one asked me to', 'I didn't understand what was involved', or even 'It always meets on Wednesday, which is my choir night'. Steps can then be taken to ensure that there are candidates next time, though it is still possible that there may be none and that the PCC will have to continue functioning below its proper strength until suitable members can be found.

The CRRs also make provision for the annual meeting to pass a resolution for electors to apply for a postal vote, in which case:

> The presiding officer shall ensure that persons who have made application for a postal vote shall be sent or have delivered a voting paper

> within 48 hours of the close of the meeting such paper to be returned to the presiding officer within such period of not less than seven days nor more than fourteen days from the date of the meeting as the presiding officer shall specify.[30]

A resolution to allow postal voting has to be approved by at least two-thirds of the people attending and entitled to vote at the annual meeting for it to become operative, and it will also not come into effect until the following year's annual meeting.

Co-opted members

Co-opted members may be ordained or lay, must be at least 16 years old and actual communicants. Co-option is for one year at a time. Co-opted members must not exceed one-fifth of the number of elected lay representatives or two persons, whichever number is the greater (see Table 4.2).

Table 4.2 Proportion of co-opted members allowed

Number of elected lay representatives	*Maximum number of co-opted members*
6	2
9	2
12	2
15	3

There are a number of reasons why a PCC might want to co-opt a member for a year. First, the PCC may be aware that it needs expertise of a certain sort, and so between elections co-opts a person who can provide the knowledge – legal, financial, architectural, etc. – that is needed. Second, there may be a member of the congregation who would make a good PCC member, but who is not sufficiently well known by those who normally attend the APCM to have a reasonable chance of being elected; a year serving on the PCC would enable them both to get a feel of the workload and responsibilities and to gain a reasonable prospect of election. Third, where there have been five candidates for four places, and all candidates would have made excellent members, the PCC might choose to co-opt the one who wasn't elected.

Filling a casual vacancy

Filling a casual vacancy may seem simple enough – a member of the PCC writes to the secretary to give apologies for the next meeting but also says that, given his failure to attend the last three meetings, he feels he should resign, and does so forthwith. It is February, and the member was almost at the end of his three-year term. What should the PCC do? The answer depends on the date of the Annual Parochial Church Meeting. Rule 48(1) of the Church Representation Rules 2006 provides that casual vacancies should be filled as soon as practicable after the vacancy occurs; and that a casual vacancy 'may be filled' by election by the PCC of a qualified person; but says that this shall not take place if the APCM is to happen 'within the next two months following the occurrence of the vacancy'. Hence, if you receive notification of a member's resignation on 16 February and your APCM is on 15 April, the filling of the vacancy should be left until the annual meeting; if your APCM is on 17 April, you may fill the casual vacancy at the next PCC meeting. The provision for a PCC member says 'may be filled' by election by the PCC; for a deanery synod member it says 'shall be filled' (though the two-month rule still applies, suggesting that the APCM should elect a deanery synod member if the vacancy falls outside the two-month period).

The relationship of PCC and DCC

The system for election to the PCC when a parish comprises several District Church Councils (DCCs) can be complicated, though need not necessarily be so. The Church Representation Rules state:

> In any parish where there are two or more churches or places of worship the annual meeting may make a scheme, which makes provision for either or both of the following purposes, that is to say:–
> (a) for the election of representatives of the laity to the parochial church council in such manner as to ensure due representation of the congregation of each such church or place; and
> (b) for the election by the annual meeting for any district in the parish in which a church or place of worship is situated of a district church council for that district.[31]

An example of (a) being fulfilled in practice is illustrated in the information provided at the website of the parish of Hednesford in the diocese of Lichfield.[32] The parish is served by three churches – St Peter's, St Saviour's and St Michael's, each of which has its own

DCC. The PCC is responsible for each of the churches within the parish, and a number of elected representatives from each church is on the PCC. Elections to DCC take place at the District Annual Meeting (DAM) of each church in the weeks leading up to the Annual Parish Meeting (APM), and in order for someone to serve on the PCC they must have been elected at a DAM. Membership of the PCC – drawn from members of the DCCs – is then confirmed at the APM. It is also possible to serve on a DCC only. The role of each DCC is to take care of the issues regarding the particular church to which it belongs, but also to 'seek to fulfil and enrich the vision and direction for the Parish offered by the PCC'.

Size of PCC

It will be seen from all the above that a PCC can vary considerably in size. The minimum size is likely to be nine (e.g. the minister, two churchwardens who are also on deanery synod, and six elected laity, with no other ex officio or co-opted members). The maximum size would be around 30 (e.g. four clergy, two churchwardens, a reader, four deanery synod members, one diocesan synod member, 15 elected lay members, and three co-opted members) in a very large parish, and even more than that in a team ministry.

♦ 5 ♦

Officers of the PCC

Chairman

The minister of the parish is the chairman of the PCC. This is the case even when the minister is not actually chairing the meeting. This may seem slightly odd given that the Parochial Church Councils (Powers) Measure 1956 states that 'it shall be the duty of the minister and the parochial church council to consult together on matters of general concern and importance to the parish', and again that one of the functions of the PCC is 'co-operation with the minister in promoting in the parish the whole mission of the Church'.

The expression 'Parochial Church Council' means the entire council, made up of ex officio, elected and co-opted members. The minister, beneficed in or licensed to the parish, is an ex officio member. The requirement 'to consult together' and to undertake 'co-operation with', as well as the wording of various other rules (e.g. the PCC 'jointly with the minister') suggest two separate entities, PCC on the one hand and minister on the other. It is this apparent separation which can give rise to a certain antagonism between minister and PCC, with the PCC coming to see itself as a sort of scrutiny committee, examining what the minister has done and giving or withholding approval. In fact the Church Representation Rules are clear that there is no separation, that the PCC is a body made up of clergy and laity, of ex officio, elected and co-opted members, and that except in rather rare circumstances there cannot be a valid meeting of the PCC without the presence of, or at least the agreement of, its chairman, the minister.

Clerical alternative chairman

There is now the possibility of another ordained person – a clerk in holy orders – who is licensed to, or has permission to officiate in, the parish being authorized by the bishop and agreeing to chair meetings of the PCC. This provision was introduced into the Synodical Government (Amendment) Measure 2003 by the Revision Committee at the suggestion of a synod member. 'It was recognized that such an arrangement might be useful in some large multi-parish benefices where there were clergy other than the minister having pastoral care of particular parishes.'[33] The application to the bishop for such authority has to be made jointly by the minister of the parish and the PCC – unless the benefice is vacant, in which case the PCC would make application alone.

This rule provides an answer to the question: 'If the vicar isn't here, can the assistant priest chair the meeting?' The answer used to be 'No' and is now 'Yes', provided that application has been made and authority granted. It might also be the case that a priest who has retired to the parish and has permission to officiate could chair the PCC during a vacancy.

Chairman presiding

This term refers to the person actually chairing or presiding over the meeting of the PCC. It should normally be the chairman (the minister) or the clerical alternative chairman (if there is one) or, if neither of these is present, the vice-chairman of the council.

The chairman presiding can vacate the chair if he or she thinks it expedient or the meeting so resolves, either for the whole meeting or for any particular item of business. If none of the three possible chairmen is available or willing to preside, the PCC can choose a person from among the members to preside for the meeting or for a particular item.

Example 1

The PCC is to discuss clergy expenses. The minister says that he will vacate the chair for this item; the clerical alternative chairman says that she must do the same. The vice-chairman is on holiday. The PCC then appoints one of its number to preside over that item, handing back to the minister for subsequent items.

Example 2

The PCC is discussing a matter concerning the fabric. None of the clergy is present and the vice-chairman, one of the churchwardens, is presiding but also needs to make a report. A member moves a resolution that the vice-chairman vacate the chair for this item; the members agree and proceed to elect a member to preside over that item.

Lay vice-chairman

A lay member of the council (who can be one of the churchwardens) must be elected as vice-chairman; an ordained person cannot be the vice-chairman. Unless there is a clerical alternative chairman (see above), then during a vacancy of the benefice, or when the chairman is absent or ill, if there is some other good reason, or when the chairman invites him or her to do so, the vice-chairman 'shall act as chairman and have all the powers vested in the chairman'.[34]

Secretary

The PCC has to have a secretary, who can be ordained or lay. The PCC may appoint one of its own members or some other fit person. If it is someone who is not a member of the council, that person does not automatically become a member, though could be co-opted (see the rules for co-option). If the person is paid for being secretary, however, they are not then eligible to be a member of the PCC.

The secretary keeps all the documents that relate to the current business of the PCC, except the electoral roll (unless he or she is also appointed electoral roll officer). He or she keeps the minutes and records all resolutions passed by the council.

It can be very useful if the secretary draws up a 'report sheet' of where the PCC is on particular issues. It can also be helpful to provide an index to the minutes, so that when issues need to be revisited, or there is an ongoing discussion about a particular issue, the relevant sections of the minutes of past meetings can be quickly and easily accessed.

The report sheet

Both new and existing members can benefit from a 'balance sheet' drawn up by the PCC secretary at the end of the year, setting out the position reached on matters discussed by the council and the implementation of the decisions it has made. It might read something like the example shown in Table 5.1.

Writing minutes

The ability to write good minutes is a particular skill, and it is one which can be honed with practice. There are certain key points to bear in mind:

Table 5.1 A report sheet

	Present position
From 2005	
Roof repairs	DAC approval; awaiting faculty; contract out to tender
Stewardship campaign	Initiated in Lent 2005; slow take-up; reviewed in November 2005 and follow-up planned but not yet undertaken
Review of mission and charity giving	Deferred until 2007
Adult education committee	Has not met; new convenor to be appointed
Kitchen decoration	Completed February 2006
Link with Russian church	Visit planned for 2007: working group to be appointed
From 2006	
Appointment of auditors	Tender document and long-list prepared; treasurer writing to six firms; Finance Committee to consider responses
Review of churchyard regulations	Under way; report to PCC in March 2007
Mission Action Plan 2007–2012	Planning group has met; report to PCC in November 2006; PCC away-day planned for early 2007

- The minutes are an official record. Sometimes formal resolutions need to be recorded. An example of this is when the PCC passes a resolution authorizing minister and churchwardens to apply for a faculty. A copy of this minute will then form part of the package to be sent to the diocesan registrar in support of the faculty application. Grant-making bodies also sometimes request to see items from the minutes, as a way of checking that an application for funding is being made on behalf of the PCC and with full PCC support. It is therefore important that minutes are not too 'chatty' and are written with a degree of formality. (It is probably better to record names in the minutes as 'Mrs Smith' and 'Mr Jones' rather than 'Sue' and 'Bob', even if that does not reflect how you actually speak to one another.)
- The names of all those present at the meeting should be included at the top of the minutes, before 'apologies for absence', which is conventionally the first item on the agenda.

- Be clear, concise and accurate. It should be possible to refer back to the minutes at a later date, if necessary, to check what was agreed or discussed, so they need to be clearly set out.
- The numbering and headings in the minutes should match those in the meeting's agenda.
- Type up the minutes from the notes you have taken during the meeting sooner rather than later. There is nothing worse than not being able to read your own notes or remember anything about what they were meant to signify!
- Keep the minutes brief, but not too brief. Minutes are not intended to be a verbatim account of a meeting – that is, you do not have to write down and reproduce every word that everyone said. You do have to ensure that all decisions are recorded, and give some indication of the process by which decisions were reached. This can be done by summarizing a discussion, or by extracting key points from it. If there is disagreement, it should be noted, though not given disproportionate space. Any votes should be recorded.
- Minute-takers often like to highlight decisions requiring actions to be taken, and by whom. Sometimes this is done in a separate 'Action' column, or sometimes the actions to be taken are re-listed together at the end of the minutes. Though this can help people remember what they have agreed to do, it is important that the minutes secretary does not appear to be bullying them, and to understand that the minutes are the formal record of a meeting, not a to-do list. If you do decide to highlight actions to be taken, remember that clarity, rather than stridency, should be the aim. It may be best to avoid **bold** or CAPITAL letters, as these can give the impression of **SHOUTING**.

Should the minutes be available to all?

The CRRs have specific rules with regard to access to past minutes:

- Minutes of meetings shall be available to all members.
- Members may have access to past minutes at the discretion of the chairman and vice-chairman if they jointly determine that they are relevant to current council business.
- The independent examiner or auditor, the bishop, the archdeacon, and any person authorized by one of them in writing may have access to the approved minutes without the council's authority.

- Other persons whose names are on the electoral roll may have access to minutes of meetings held after the APCM of 1995 except any deemed by the council to be confidential.
- Persons other than those whose names are on the electoral roll may have access to the minutes only in accordance with the specific authorization of the council (unless they have been deposited in the diocesan record office).

> St Paul after reading all these rules? *We are perplexed, but not in despair.* [2 Corinthians 4.8]

If the minutes are to be really useful, they should be considered as working documents for members. To deal with access by non-members who are nevertheless on the electoral roll, they should be divided into 'public' and 'confidential'. An edited version of the minutes could be displayed on the notice-board or posted on the website, omitting sensitive or confidential material, but it is probably better to provide a summary report to the congregation.

Treasurer

The PCC shall have a treasurer or more than one treasurer, acting jointly. The CRRs recognize that there can be difficulties in finding a treasurer and a number of alternative scenarios is offered, in order of preference:

1. A member of the PCC should be appointed as sole treasurer, or two or more members can be appointed jointly. If this proves impossible, then –
2. The office can be discharged by a churchwarden. If neither churchwarden is willing or able to discharge the office, then –
3. Some other fit person, who is not a member of the PCC, may be appointed. That person is eligible for co-option to the PCC, under the co-option rules, with one exception. If the PCC pays the treasurer, then he or she is not eligible to be a member of the council in any category, ex officio, elected or co-opted.

Electoral roll officer

Every parish is required to have a church electoral roll. This is not in any way to be confused with the register of electors maintained by the local authority and used for local and parliamentary elections. The church electoral roll is, essentially, a membership roll. The PCC is required to appoint an electoral roll officer 'who may but need not be a member of the council and may be the secretary'.[35] The electoral roll officer may be paid, if the PCC thinks fit, but only if he or she is not a member of the PCC. The officer has charge of the roll but acts under the direction of the PCC (CRRs Rule 1[7]). This means that he or she keeps the roll up to date by addition or removal of names according to the rules, and reports the additions and removals to the PCC at the next meeting. Whenever additions and/or removals are made, a list of all those added or removed has to be 'published by being exhibited continuously for not less than fourteen days on or near the principal door of every church in the parish . . . in such manner as the council may appoint'.[36] The purpose of the display of the roll is so that members may ascertain if they have been included on it as requested. It is not intended to be a parish directory where people can look up addresses. Indeed it is now generally agreed that it is not sensible, and may even be a violation of the Data Protection Act 1998, to display lists of names and addresses on the church notice-board. If some indication of address is needed to differentiate between people of similar name, then a postcode could be printed rather than a full address.

The electoral roll officer is to keep the roll and make it available for inspection by bona fide enquirers – that is, anyone who is either resident in the parish or named on the electoral roll. The CRRs note, however, that 'the secretary shall not be bound to provide a copy of such list'.[37]

The electoral roll is important because it provides the basis for qualification for lay office in the church (as churchwarden, member of the PCC, member of deanery synod etc.) and for qualification to vote. It is a list of lay members; the clergy may not be on an electoral roll. To be eligible for enrolment, a lay person must be baptized, be 16 years of age or upwards, and have signed an application form on which he or she declares one of three things:

1 he or she is a member of the Church of England or of a Church in communion with it and resides in the parish; or
2 he or she is a member of the Church of England or of a Church in communion with it and, not being resident in the parish, has habitually attended public worship in the parish during the six months prior to enrolment; or

3 he or she is not a member of the Church of England or of a Church in communion with it, but is a member in good standing of some other Church which subscribes to the doctrine of the Holy Trinity and declares him- or herself to be a member of the Church of England having habitually attended public worship in the parish during the six months prior to enrolment.

What does this mean in practice?

Example 1: the unbaptized

Chris Knight came regularly to Evensong at St Faith's. Seeing him there most weeks, the churchwardens thought he would be a good sidesman but noticed he was not on the roll. They asked him to complete a form but he said, 'I am not baptized!' He cannot therefore be entered on the roll or be a sidesman.

Example 2: the clergy

The Revd John Hall had retired to the parish of St Mary Magdalene. He was rather unsteady on his legs and never assisted with services, but was usually present in the congregation. The electoral roll officer invited him to join the roll but Mr Hall pointed out that it was a list of lay people and he was not eligible to be enrolled.

Example 3: resident parishioners

The residents of Mulberry Close, a small estate within the parish, were opposed to plans to extend the church hall on land behind their houses. All 12 of them decided to join the roll of their parish church, in order to seek election to the PCC, although none of them ever went to services there. They asked the electoral roll officer for forms. As the roll was very small, it was clear that, if they all turned up to the APCM, this group of residents would form a substantial majority. The electoral roll officer asked the vicar whether they were entitled to be enrolled and he said, 'Yes, as long as they are baptized, over 16, and are members of the Church of England.'

Example 4: habitual worship

'How often is habitual?' asked Tracy Smith, who wanted to get married at St Mary's next year but lived in the next-door parish. 'Does it mean every week?'

'No,' said the vicar, 'it has no precise definition. Once a month for six months would do to qualify, but I would rather that you came more often than that.'

'And can I come to a week-day service rather than one on Sunday?'

'Yes, you can. Any of our services will do; all of them are "public worship".'

Example 5: in communion with the Church of England

Erik came from Sweden to live in the parish of St Winifred. He was a member of the Swedish Lutheran Church but worshipped regularly with the Anglican congregation.

'Join our electoral roll,' said the churchwardens.

'I can't,' said Erik, 'I am a Lutheran.'

He was very surprised when the churchwardens told him that the Swedish Church was in communion with the Church of England and he could be enrolled.

Example 6: in good standing

Paul and Mary were life-long Methodists but the chapel in their village had closed and, although they drove the five miles to the church in the town for morning service three times a month, they worshipped at the parish church in the evening. They were delighted to be invited to join the electoral roll of the parish.

The electoral roll officer not only enters names on to the list, but also removes them. Some will be removed because they ask to be or because they are moving away, but those qualified under habitual attendance at public worship can be disqualified if they cease to be habitual worshippers. The CRRs give six categories of people who should be removed:

1 The dead.
2 Those who become ordained.
3 Those who ask to be removed.
4 Those who cease to reside in the parish and do not habitually attend public worship there.
5 Those not resident in the parish who have not habitually attended public worship in the parish during the preceding six months.
6 Those who should not have been entered on the roll originally.

The rules do allow one exception to categories (4) or (5) – those who are prevented by illness or some other sufficient cause from attending public worship. When the electoral roll officer posts a list of those removed from a parish roll, it must contain notification of the right of appeal against removal. This right is contained in CRRs Rule 43 and provides that an appeal against refused enrolment or removal from the roll may be made in writing to the lay chairman of the deanery synod not later than 14 days after the list was posted. If such an appeal is lodged, the lay chairman is required to refer it to the Bishop's Council! A person whose name is on the roll may also object either to the enrolment or the removal of the name of any other person on that roll. Three examples may help to illustrate these rules.

Example 7: a sufficient cause

Annie had lived in the parish since she was a girl, but at 85 years of age she went to live with her son 15 miles away. As he worked on Sundays she could get to church only very infrequently, but she came when she could and continued as a member of the stewardship scheme. The electoral roll officer took her case to the PCC and the members decided that she was prevented from attending by a sufficient cause, and resolved to keep her on the roll.

Example 8: removal for non-attendance

Ralph MacDonald was a long-time opponent of the vicar's, and indeed of the vicar before him. He delighted in asking unhelpful questions at the APCM and bombarded the archdeacon with complaints. He did not live in the parish but attended Evensong every two or three weeks, arriving late and causing a fuss. After a particularly heated argument with the vicar, he wrote his usual letter of complaint, and was not seen in church for three or four weeks. A month of absence extended to six months, and the churchwardens counted every week until they realized he was disqualified. The electoral roll officer removed his name from the roll and displayed a notice showing that Mr MacDonald's name, along with several others, had been removed. The notice contained the words: 'Those whose names are removed from the Electoral Roll of this Parish have a right of appeal under Rule 43 of the Church Representation Rules 2006.' Mr MacDonald did not appeal.

Example 9: an objection

Tracy Smith knew that she needed to attend public worship habitually in order to be entered on the roll and be enabled to marry at St Mary's, but somehow she only managed to get there four times in six months. Nevertheless she filled in her enrolment form and her name went up on the board. So did that of another bride-to-be, Ellen Pickard, but she had made a point of coming to the Parish

Eucharist every Sunday. Mrs Courtney, a member of St Mary's PCC, was opposed to the roll being used for this purpose and had often spoken against it. When she saw the names go up on the board, she immediately lodged an objection with the lay chairman of the deanery synod under Rule 43. The lay chairman passed the appeal to the Bishop's Council. Three lay members of the council were appointed to consider and decide the appeal. They ruled that Tracy could not be enrolled, but Ellen could. Mrs Courtney was satisfied.

The roll has to be revised every year in the month leading up to the annual meeting (specifically, 'not less than fifteen days or more than twenty-eight days'[38] before the meeting). A notice announcing that this revision shall take place must be displayed 'on or near the principal door of every church in the parish and every building in the parish licensed for public worship'[39] for not less than a fortnight before the revision begins. When the revised roll, which takes into account all additions and removals made during the year, has been completed, it must likewise be displayed, along with a list of all those who have been removed from the roll since the last revision, for at least a fortnight before the annual meeting. Any errors or omissions can now be brought to the attention of the electoral roll officer and rectified, but no further new additions or removals can take place until after the annual meeting.

Every six years (unless a variation of the six-year rule has been decreed as it has for 2007, the last preparation of new rolls having taken place in 2002), the electoral roll must be completely redone. A notice stating that a new roll is to be prepared has to be displayed at least two months before the annual meeting of the relevant year (2007 is the next one), and an announcement about it also has to be made during services in church on the two Sundays after the notice has gone up. (In practice the announcement will probably go on being made throughout the two-month period, in order to remind people to fill in their forms.) Everyone who was on the previous roll and who wishes, and is entitled, to be entered on the new one must now fill in a form. The new roll must be completed 'not less than fifteen days or more than twenty-eight days'[40] before the annual meeting. Again it must now be displayed 'on or near the principal door of the parish church'[41] for at least a fortnight, during which time any errors or omissions can be corrected, but no new names can be added or any deleted until after the close of the annual meeting.

♦ 6 ♦

Meetings of the PCC

Clause nine of the Parochial Church Councils (Powers) Measure 1921 attached a Schedule to the Measure containing rules of procedure for the council, but allowing amendment with the consent of a higher body (the diocesan conference, now superseded by the diocesan synod), and allowing the council to make bylaws to regulate procedure as long as the bylaws were not inconsistent with superior rules, regulations and measures. The Schedule dealt with the power to call meetings, notices, quorum and agenda, etc., all of which, though some in modified form, are familiar from the current rules.

Frequency

There have to be at least four meetings of the PCC a year, but in a busy parish there are likely to be more. The busiest of parishes will, however, rarely require more than six, unless some major project is under way when a monthly PCC meeting may be necessary. If no more than four meetings are held, they should as far as possible take place at quarterly intervals. Meetings must also not be too lengthy and it can be better to have a PCC away-day, with less formal discussion of parish matters, than to have a series of over-long and over-burdened regular meetings.

Calling a meeting

The chairman (i.e. the minister) convenes the meeting by displaying a notice specifying the time and place at or near the principal door of every church in the parish, at least ten clear days before the meeting. (In practice the PCC secretary probably does this and members will have been informed of the planned meeting dates a considerable time in advance.) The notice must be signed by or on behalf of the chairman. It is possible to postpone a convened meeting for up to a fortnight 'for some good and sufficient reason'.[42]

If one third of the membership of the PCC signs a requisition asking the minister to call a meeting, he or she must do so within seven days (or, if the minister fails to do so, they can convene a meeting themselves). A meeting convened in this way will still be an ordinary meeting of the PCC, chaired according to the normal rules – that is, the minister chairs the meetings as usual, or the alternative clerical chairman does, or the vice-chairman, or a member elected by the meeting. The members cannot simply have a meeting without the minister; only if the minister is absent, or asks the vice-chairman to take the chair, is he or she not the chairman.

Quorum

The quorum for a valid meeting of the PCC is one third of its members, drawn from any of the three categories of membership.

Emergency meetings

An emergency is a sudden unforeseen crisis that requires immediate action. For the PCC this might include substantial damage to the church building caused by storm, fire or explosion; the unexpected failure of the organ; the discovery of theft, fraud or deception; or something of that sort. There may be other 'special circumstances' that require immediate action by the council, and that may be as simple as the urgent but unexpected need to change a bank mandate if someone is involved in an accident or dies suddenly. In these circumstances the chairman, but only the chairman, can convene a meeting, giving three clear days' notice and specifying in the notice the business to be transacted. A quorum to enable the business to be transacted is a majority of the then existing members of the council – e.g. if there are nine members, there must be five at the meeting; if there are 30 members, there must be 16 at the meeting. No business other than that set out in the convening notice can be transacted.

Extraordinary meetings

There is one further type of meeting of the PCC: the extraordinary meeting. Although the CRRs do not specifically say so, this is the sort of meeting that is called to consider pastoral breakdown. It is convened by the archdeacon if one third of the lay members of the

PCC or one tenth of the persons on the electoral roll ask for it and have given, in the judgement of the archdeacon, sufficient cause. The archdeacon is the sole judge of whether the cause is sufficient, but he or she will certainly want to know that every other avenue has been explored and will also want to know why the members of the council have not themselves convened a meeting under the powers they have under the General Provisions Relating to Parochial Church Councils[43] (see 'Calling a meeting' above). An extraordinary meeting differs from an ordinary meeting, however convened, and an emergency meeting, in that the archdeacon either chairs it or appoints a chairman. Unless the chairman is a member of the PCC, he or she has neither a first vote nor a casting vote. The minister, as a member of the PCC, is entitled to attend, speak and vote, but not to chair the meeting (unless appointed to do so).

Why, then, would members ask for an extraordinary meeting? The simplest answer is the sort of breakdown, within the PCC and between the PCC and the minister or officers, which requires extraordinary action, with the hope that the archdeacon will be able to help to sort the matter out. There is no provision for any variation of the general rules that apply to PCCs, and so the ordinary rules as to the convening notice, agenda and quorum apply.

Types of business

There are various types of business which may need to be covered in a PCC meeting, or over a series of several meetings.

The main business of the PCC concerns the setting of its strategic direction and the fulfilling of objectives stemming from its overall policy. This may be worked out in a mission statement, mission action plan or parish plan, or may be set by the job description and person specification drawn up for the incumbent or priest-in-charge. There will need to be coherence between the parish's strategic direction and diocesan policy.

Then there is the business of the PCC which implements this overall policy and strategic direction; such business is often of a financial nature. Secondary questions may arise which can be judged in accordance with the overall policy. Examples of such questions would be:

- How does the diocesan Lent appeal fit with our main policy?
- Is the request of a choir to rehearse in the church every Tuesday evening in line with our policy on the use of the church building?

A third type of business concerns matters which are divorced from the main policy and on which there may be a diversity of views. Examples could include some issues to do with the churchyard, or the possibility of a filming project.

Then there are issues sent down for discussion from deanery or diocesan level. There can also be matters to discuss of wider church or community interest – from ecumenical questions to issues over parking or licensing. There may be issues concerning which the minister would like to know what PCC members think, even though the decision may not be theirs to make. There can be new initiatives, new situations presenting unexpected questions, matters which have never arisen before.

Quite apart from all these varieties of formal business, PCCs can also benefit from some time together for the 'informal business' of getting to know one another better in a social and less time-pressured setting than a formal meeting will allow.

Agenda

In the case of ordinary scheduled meetings, in addition to the convening notice displayed at least ten days beforehand, a notice with an agenda should be sent to members seven days before the meeting is to take place. (It can be posted seven days before, rather than having to arrive seven days before the meeting; it can be sent by e-mail, provided members have agreed to this.) This notice is to be signed by or on behalf of the secretary. The CRRs state that the notice shall contain 'the agenda of the meeting including any motion or other business proposed by any member of the council of which notice has been received by the secretary'.[44] These rules do not apply to the meeting of the PCC that immediately follows the APCM (at which the only business is the election of officers and a standing committee).

The rules do not state how the content of the agenda is determined, but only items of business specified on the agenda are to be transacted at the meeting unless three quarters of the members present consent to another item being introduced. The business is to be taken in the order set down on the agenda, unless the council resolves to alter the order.

It is helpful to have an annual schedule that indicates the matters that must be dealt with at a given meeting, and it can also be useful to have a timetable for major annual business, such as the setting of the budget and the receipt of the annual report and accounts.

Table 6.1 An annual business timetable

April – after APCM	Elect vice-chairman Elect treasurer Elect secretary Elect electoral roll officer Elect standing committee
May	Discuss church fête arrangements
July	Half-year budget review
September	Set dates for next year's PCC meetings and APCM
October	*Receive draft budget from treasurer*
November	Receive draft budget from standing committee Review Mission Action Plan targets
January	*Revise budget as necessary*
January	Agree final version of budget (Nominations for missionary and charitable giving should be made to the standing committee not later than the January PCC meeting so as to be considered at the February meeting of the committee)
February	*Consider draft annual report* *Prepare recommendations for nomination to PCC* *Prepare recommendations for missionary and charitable giving*
March	Agree annual report and financial statements for APCM Agree missionary and charitable giving
	Standing committee in italics

The form of the agenda is then determined in any way that the PCC decides: this could be by the chairman alone; by the chairman and secretary; by the chairman, vice-chairman and secretary; by church officers; or by the standing committee.

Any meeting will begin in prayer and then include apologies for absence, approval of minutes of the previous meeting, and matters arising from the minutes not covered elsewhere in the agenda. Regular items may include secretary's business or items that the chairman needs to report on (and which may even have arisen since the agenda was prepared). The core business of the meeting will then be addressed, possibly with reports on finance and fabric and from committees, or consideration of matters referred to the PCC by the diocese.

Some prayers for PCC meetings

Diversity of gifts

Lord of the Church, who hast given to thy servants a diversity of gifts, that they may share them with their brethren; Grant us the generous heart to give, the humble heart to receive; that we, with all that love thee, may know the fullness of thy grace; that thy love may be perfected in us; to the glory of thy Name.

For the diocese

O God, by your grace you have called us in this Diocese to a goodly fellowship of faith. Bless our Bishop *N.* and other clergy, and all our people. Grant that your Word may be truly preached and truly heard, your Sacraments faithfully administered and faithfully received. By your Spirit, fashion our lives according to the example of your Son, and grant that we may show the power of your love to all among whom we live; through Jesus Christ our Lord.

For the parish

Almighty and everliving God, ruler of all things in heaven and earth, hear our prayers for this parish family. Strengthen the faithful, arouse the careless, and restore the penitent. Grant us all things necessary for our common life, and bring us all to be of one heart and mind within your holy Church; through Jesus Christ our Lord.

The agenda may include an item such as 'Questions concerning the work of the council'. Such questions may be invited verbally or in writing. There must be an understanding that, unless there has been sufficient advance notice, it may not be possible to give an answer at that meeting.

Meetings sometimes conclude with 'Any other business' (AOB), but there are good reasons for not including this. Members sometimes use AOB to raise issues, late in the day, that are too large for consideration there and then, and AOB is a regular haunt of the 'fjord-raider' (see pp. 86–7) hoping to ambush the minister, churchwardens or treasurer. If there is going to be AOB, it needs to be either 'any other business of which advance notice has been given to the Chairman not less than 24 hours before the meeting' or an opportunity to flag up issues for future discussion.

The CRRs refer to the inclusion of 'any motion or other business proposed by any member of the council of which notice has been received by the secretary'.[45] Does this in fact mean that members determine the content of the agenda, and that any item they propose must be included? It might seem that it does, but if this were the case the regular business of the PCC could easily be derailed by one or two vociferous members. The broad sweep of business to be discussed by the PCC is determined by two things – its statutory and legal obligations, and the overall parish vision or strategy. The preparation of the statement containing the vision or strategy must allow for ample opportunity for the discussion of diverse views. Once certain options have been accepted and others rejected, the general pattern is set for the three- to five-year period, and attempts to derail the strategy would be counterproductive. The officers of the PCC have a duty to promote the agreed strategy and to discourage the regular appearance of motions that would frustrate this.

These sorts of motions can be dealt with procedurally by a resolution that the council 'move to the next business' (i.e. pass on to the next agenda item without further consideration or a vote on the motion) but it is probably better, except as a last resort, to show that the matter will be dealt with at an appropriate time. Here are some examples of things that might be brought to PCC, and the sort of response officers might give:

'I disagree very strongly with what the bishop has said about homosexuality and I would like to move a motion condemning it.'
Response: Such a motion would be *ultra vires* (i.e. outside the powers of the PCC). It is possible to discuss the matter but not to pass any resolution.

'I have noticed water dripping in the north transept. I would like to have a discussion about the state of the fabric.'
Response: The churchwardens are aware of the leak but it cannot be dealt with until the scaffolding is erected for the work on the tower. It will be mentioned in their annual report on fabric.

'I am very much opposed to the ordination of women and I propose that the PCC should pass Resolutions A and B and seek alternative episcopal oversight.'
Response: This was considered at the time of the ordination of women to the priesthood and rejected. It has been considered twice since, with the same result. It will be discussed again after the PCC elections in April.

'I don't agree with the way in which the proceeds of the church bazaar are distributed and I want to discuss it in PCC.'
Response: The distribution of moneys is agreed annually by the PCC on the recommendation of the away-giving committee. There is a chance to discuss it then.

'May we please have a discussion about the hymns? I don't know who chooses them but they have been quite unsingable lately.'
Response: The hymns, and indeed most other aspects of worship, do not fall within the authority of the PCC. The hymns and other musical items are chosen by the minister with the advice of the organist.

Changing the rules

The provisions in the CRRs for setting the agenda are clearly inadequate; but can they be changed? Rule 15, to which the General Provisions are attached, provides that 'a parochial church council may, with the consent of the diocesan synod, vary the said provisions, in their application to the council'.[46] It would therefore be possible to propose to the synod an amendment of Section 4 of the General Provisions, such as the following one (amended text in italics):

> Not less than seven days before the meeting a notice thereof specifying the time and place of the meeting signed by or on behalf of the secretary shall be posted or delivered to every member of the council. Such notice shall contain the agenda of the meeting, *which shall have been agreed by the chairman, vice-chairman and secretary, after considering any motion or other item proposed by a member for inclusion in the agenda of which notice has been given to the secretary.*

Ambushes and fjord-raiders

Meeting the PCC secretary for tea prior to the meeting, the vicar observed that it looked like a straightforward agenda and that they ought to make some progress on the new vicarage and the stewardship campaign. The reports on both matters had been circulated to members. At 7.30 p.m. the vicar opened the meeting with prayers, took the apologies for absence, welcomed back a member who had been ill, had the minutes agreed and asked: 'Are there any matters arising from the minutes that are not covered elsewhere in the agenda?'

Mrs Ketley said 'Yes!' and produced a nine-page document concerning the future of the Sunday school, which she passed around.

The vicar scanned it quickly; his sigh was probably audible. Every word he had ever spoken on the question of the Sunday school, especially every negative word, had, it seemed, been written down and incorporated into this paper. 'It would not, I think, be appropriate to discuss this now, given that we have only just seen it,' he ventured cautiously, hoping for support from other members.

'But I insist,' said Mrs Ketley. 'I find the whole thing very upsetting and your attitude, Vicar, very unhelpful, and we really must resolve it.'

As no one came to his rescue, the vicar suggested that the paper might be considered at the end, and so it was, in a discussion that lasted from 9.45 p.m. to nearly 11 o'clock, and which was recorded by the PCC secretary as a heated discussion between the vicar and Mrs Ketley.

It was an ambush. Whether other members of the PCC knew it was going to happen and allowed it, or not, was not entirely clear, but the vicar was put in a very difficult position and it is not surprising that the matter became heated. When, at about 10.15 p.m., he whispered to the PCC secretary, 'I'm going to the loo' and left the room, many thought he had said, 'I'm going home.' Who could have blamed him? As it was, the next few days were spent in patching up the damage and exchanging letters of apology.

Another way of thinking of this sort of unscheduled business is as a fjord-raider – a warship that emerges unexpectedly from a fjord to attack commercial vessels. The PCC meeting has been carefully prepared to ensure that the business of the PCC is carried through. The raider attempts to capture the meeting and divert it to his or her own purposes. Whether an ambush or a raid, behaviour of this sort is contrary to the PCC's Christian spirituality – because it shows no respect for the council, the chairman or its members – and is ultimately counterproductive. It prevents the proper business of the PCC being carried through. Where the PCC's officers have taken the trouble to listen to the membership and to provide a means by which matters can find a proper place on the agenda, ambushes and fjord-raiding cannot be tolerated. The responsibility for preventing such action rests on the whole PCC and not just on the officers.

Should the agenda be available to all?

There is no reason why the PCC agenda should not be made public but, in that case, sensitive or confidential matters should not be identified. This makes the agenda less useful and it is probably better to keep it as a working document for PCC members.

Attendance

In addition to members of the council, members of lay staff (an administrator, for example) or the PCC's professional advisers may attend PCC meetings with the consent, or at the invitation of, the council.

Should the PCC be open to any member of the parish or congregation or the press?

There is no requirement for PCC meetings to be held in public; indeed, public attendance is not mentioned in the rules governing the working of the PCC. Though transparency and accountability in decision-making is to be encouraged, the members of a PCC may often need time to consider the arguments for and against a proposed course of action, and the presence of non-members can discourage wide-ranging and open-ended discussion. There may also be occasions when the PCC is to consider sensitive or confidential material and it is clear that non-members should not be present at all on those occasions.

The CRRs make provision for special parochial church meetings, and there may be matters that would be conveniently dealt with by summoning such a meeting which is open only to lay persons whose names appear on the church electoral roll (and did so 21 clear days before the meeting) together with such clergy as are eligible to attend the annual parish meeting.

Confidentiality

Certain matters are necessarily confidential. These will always include specific references to certain personal circumstances of members of the council or church (e.g. ill health, legal problems, marital relations, financial situation), and details of the remuneration and conduct of employees. Other matters may be deemed confidential, and these might include the management accounts, certain proposals that are under consideration but are not yet ready to be made public, and critical observations about the diocese, neighbouring parishes, etc. It will be for the chairman to guide the meeting, but he or she must make it clear when an item is confidential and why.

Given the possibility of access to non-confidential minutes, the PCC minutes will need to have 'Part II minutes' that are clearly marked 'Confidential' and are stored separately from the other minutes. The 'Part I' minutes can indicate that confidential minutes exist.

The minister needs to feel that he or she can trust the PCC, and that the members will respect a request for confidentiality. (If this trust is lacking, the most likely outcome is that the minister will cease confiding in the PCC, which will be to everyone's detriment.)

Voting procedures

A majority vote decides business, and in an equal division of votes the chairman has the second or casting vote. How should the casting vote be used? There are two views on this. The first is that the chairman should vote in a way that keeps the debate open, which normally means voting against the change that is proposed and in favour of the status quo, whatever his or her own convictions. The second is that the chairman's casting vote should be exercised in whichever way he or she thinks appropriate. That is to say, it is a genuine vote and the chairman can cast it in exactly the way he or she cast the first vote, if that was a genuine expression of his or her view. If the chairman can vote only for the status quo, then the casting vote is of no use.

The good PCC meeting

So much for all the rules and regulations. What features will mark the best sort of PCC meeting?

> St Paul on the perfect PCC meeting? *Now I beseech you, brethren, by the name of our Lord Jesus Christ, that ye all speak the same thing, and that there be no divisions among you; but that ye be perfectly joined together in the same mind and in the same judgment.* [1 Corinthians 1.10]

Characteristics of the good PCC meeting

- **It is not too long.** If properly organized and prepared, most meetings should be able to be concluded within the space of two hours.

There may be the occasional meeting which lasts longer than this, but if meetings regularly go on longer then the agenda may be overloaded and it might be better to have more, shorter, meetings. Otherwise people may become tired and fractious.

- **Everyone speaks, but no one speaks too much.** It is important that everyone's voice is heard, and that no one voice is allowed to dominate the meeting. If some people are initially reluctant to speak, it may help if the chairman deliberately asks each person round the table to give their opinion on a particular issue, even if it is only to agree with the majority view. If someone is trying to talk all the time, the same technique can be employed, this time with a specific time limit – perhaps using a kitchen timer – being set for everyone to keep to.
- **It keeps to the agenda.** The discussion is restricted to what has actually been set for the meeting.
- **There is a clear procedure for how to get items on to the agenda.** Sticking to the agenda is more likely to be managed if members feel assured that the agenda accurately reflects the business that needs to be transacted at this point, and that other matters of concern will be given an appropriate time slot in the future. Rather than falling into the potential morass of 'any other business', members can be given the opportunity to flag up issues which they would like to be included in a future agenda.
- **Briefing papers have been read and preparation done.** When members have read any written material distributed in advance of the meeting and have considered what they have been asked to consider between meetings, the meeting is more likely to be both efficient and productive.
- **Old issues are not endlessly revisited.** Where decisions have already been made, and they are not scheduled to be revisited, it should be politely but firmly pointed out (perhaps by the secretary) to anyone attempting to revive an earlier discussion that this issue is now closed and it is time to move on.
- **No one is allowed to sidetrack the meeting.** Most groups of people can boast at least one member who enjoys telling long-winded anecdotes or simply finds it very hard to keep to the point. All members should play their part in discouraging irrelevant rambling.
- **There are no separate meetings going on.** No meeting can be satisfactorily conducted if there is more than one meeting going on at a time – i.e. if a small group of people down one end of the

table are muttering and whispering together, instead of contributing to the general discussion.

- **Opinions are aired at the meeting, not afterwards.** If everyone is given a chance to speak, and avails themselves of it, then no one should leave a meeting feeling they have not been heard. It can be a great waste of everyone's time, and does not contribute to harmony, if there are some members who refuse to speak at a meeting and then go and complain about issues and other people afterwards, either in a private group or by firing off cross e-mails to churchwardens, secretary or minister.
- **Humour is allowed.** Despatching business efficiently does not mean there is no place for laughter.
- **There is prayer, but the meeting does not become a Bible study.** Opening and closing prayers help to anchor the meeting and foster the sense of playing a part in the overall mission of the church. The PCC meeting is not, however, a prayer meeting or a Bible study and it shouldn't feel like one. In particular, no one, including the chairman, should be allowed to use prayer as a means of manipulating others, by implying there is divine approval for one's own point of view.
- **There is no fear of leaks.** When confidential items are discussed – and recorded in confidential minutes – there should be an absolute understanding that confidentiality will be respected.
- **Disagreement can be expressed without animosity.** It should be possible to disagree, even disagree strongly, with one another without that disagreement becoming an occasion for personal animosity. When a body is united in its objectives, there may still be disagreement over precisely how to attain those objectives. No one should feel under personal attack if they hold to a minority view; neither should they allow themselves to feel resentful.
- **Failure (of ourselves and others) is forgiven.** Given that a degree of maturity is needed to manage disagreement, and that none of us is perfect or behaves maturely all the time, past upsets should be learnt from and forgiven. A run of good PCC meetings may often be followed by a difficult one, and we should not get too exercised about the occasional difficulty.
- **The members, as well as the chairman, take responsibility for the conduct of the meeting.** A mature approach demands collective 'ownership' of the meeting, a collective determination that it should conduct its business efficiently and properly. So, for instance, if you are aware that a 'cabal' of potential discontents is in danger

of forming at one end of the table, you can tactfully break it up by going to sit there at the start of the meeting. Or if you notice a new member is finding it hard to summon up the courage to speak, you can take the time between meetings to get to know him or her better and explain some of the procedures and how you felt when you first joined. If one individual tries to derail the meeting, members do not need to wait for the chairman to intervene, but can propose a motion to move to the next item of business.

- **The meeting is consonant with the whole mission of the church.** The fact that the PCC has business to conduct at its meetings and must conform with the regulations does not mean that the meeting is somehow separate from the rest of the church's life. Members should be able to feel that by transacting the necessary business efficiently and well, they are helping to take forward the whole work of the church, and that both the large and small issues they deal with and the decisions they reach are in line with the overall mission of the parish. (See Chapter 2 on 'Is there a spirituality appropriate to the PCC?)

Electronic communication

The use of electronic communication can be of great help in conducting PCC business but here, as in other areas of life, it can also contain pitfalls. A disciplined approach is needed when using e-mail. It can save money – if, for instance, agenda, minutes and other papers are distributed electronically whenever possible – and it can on occasion speed up decision-making (if there is a straightforward matter which needs to be decided quickly at a time when a PCC meeting is not scheduled). But it also carries the temptation to indulge in ad-hoc discussions which should properly be conducted in the context of a meeting, and to do so in an inflammatory manner. Things to avoid include:

- firing off e-mails when you're feeling tired and cross (remember you can't call them back once you've pressed 'send');
- copying everyone into an e-mail so that they can all see the criticism you're directing at minister or churchwardens;
- continually using e-mail to ask questions which may be time-consuming for the minister, churchwardens or church staff to answer;
- expecting, and demanding, an immediate reply.

You should not use e-mail to try to conduct a quasi-PCC meeting outside of the meeting. For one thing, it should be remembered that not everyone has e-mail or feels at ease using this medium, so that you are in danger of excluding some people if you engage in discussion by e-mail. But of course e-mail is of immense value when it comes to routine jobs, such as arranging rotas and so on.

> St Paul on cross e-mails? *Be not deceived: evil communications corrupt good manners.* [1 Corinthians 15.33]

How to be a really difficult member of the PCC

1. Ensure that you have copies of the Parochial Church Council (Powers) Measure 1956, the Church Representation Rules in their most up-to-date version, the document *The Charities Act 1993 and the PCC*, the Canons of the Church of England, and all the measures available on the Office of Public Sector Information (OPSI) website that affect the parish or the clergy.
2. Visit the website of the Ecclesiastical Law Society, look at the cases reported there, and see if any of them provide ammunition for tripping up the minister and churchwardens.
3. Keep careful note of failure to comply with any regulation, especially failure to put up notices at the right time or in the right place.
4. Inform the secretary in advance of a number of matters you want discussed and resolutions that you want to put to the meeting.
5. Raise points of order during the meeting and suggest as often as you can that proper procedures have not been followed in the preliminaries to the meeting or in the meeting itself.
6. Prepare a number of questions prior to the discussion of every financial report and query different categories of expenditure at each meeting.
7. Insist that the names of those being added to or removed from the electoral roll be read out at the PCC meeting; ask questions about them and oppose additions and deletions alternately.
8. Think of all the reasons why any proposal being put to the PCC is wrong, and argue your case at the meeting, while constantly pleading that you have probably misunderstood it all anyway.
9. Vote against anything proposed by the chairman, and insist that your dissenting vote be recorded.

10 Send letters or e-mails after a PCC meeting asking for clarification of matters that you could have asked about at the meeting, but deliberately didn't.
11 Complain when you don't get an immediate reply.
12 Copy letters and e-mails to all members of the PCC and to the area/rural dean, the lay chairman of the deanery synod and the archdeacon.
13 Oppose faculty applications for anything and everything both in the meeting and by formal objection to the diocesan registrar.
14 When something does go wrong, latch on to it, express concern, ask lots of questions, and insist on seeing letters and papers, saying that you are only trying to be a conscientious member of the PCC.
15 Tell the churchwardens that people are saying that PCC members are all yes-men, are concerned about the minister's behaviour, dislike the style of services, etc. Refuse to name names because you have been told in confidence.
16 Suggest, to anyone who cares to listen, that all is not well in the parish.
17 Refuse to meet with the minister or churchwardens to discuss any of your concerns, because you are too busy.
18 Accuse the minister and churchwardens of bullying or intimidatory behaviour.
19 Write to the bishop or archdeacon from time to time to protest about some change or to complain about something – anything will do. Always apologize for your protest or complaint, say you make it with a heavy heart, and in a spirit of Christian charity.
20 Write to the bishop or archdeacon complaining that you have not received a reply to your letter. Copy it to the archbishop.
21 If all else fails, cancel your standing order to the PCC or membership of stewardship (if you didn't oppose the minister's insistence that all PCC members be in stewardship) and announce, to all willing to hear, that this was not the church you joined, that you are leaving, that you hope your faith will be restored somewhere else, and that you might return when the current minister has gone. Write to the bishop (copy to the archbishop) to tell him what you have done and why.
22 Move to another parish; start again.

If the PCC is faced with a really difficult member (even if not quite as difficult as the one envisaged above!), then again the problem can only be satisfactorily dealt with collectively. If the difficult person is made to realize they are annoying the whole council with their disruptive tactics, rather than just the minister (who is very probably the real target), they may – possibly – consider it best to desist. In particular, members should not inadvertently fall in with the 'difficult one's' plans, by joining in malicious gossip or moaning about meetings or other members or whatever. And in a meeting do not always wait for the chairman to call a difficult member to order – particularly as this is what the difficult member wants to happen, so that he or she will have yet another reason to be disgruntled, yet another stick to beat the minister with.

♦ 7 ♦

Working with others

Working with the minister

We have already covered much of how a PCC should work with its chairman, but it may be helpful at this point to summarize the specific duties of the minister and to present a picture of the ideal chairman!

Duties of the minister

1. To celebrate the Eucharist (or cause it to be celebrated in his or her absence) and administer the other rites and sacraments of the Church.
2. To be responsible for liturgy.
3. To have ultimate responsibility for music performed during the liturgy, in co-operation with the director of music, organist or choirmaster.
4. To preach (or cause to be preached) at least one sermon every Sunday.
5. To instruct parishioners in the Christian faith.
6. To prepare candidates for confirmation.
7. To visit the sick.
8. To be prepared to make himself or herself available to parishioners seeking spiritual counsel and advice.
9. To be diligent in prayer and study.
10. To chair the PCC, the PCC standing committee and the APCM.
11. To consult with the PCC.
12. To co-operate with the churchwardens.

Characteristics of the good PCC chairman

Some of these are a logical corollary to 'Characteristics of a good PCC meeting' and many of them are a question of getting the balance right.

- He or she knows the rules, but doesn't use that knowledge as a weapon.
- He or she speaks clearly and firmly, but doesn't shout.

- He or she knows how to listen.
- He or she does not become defensive in the face of disagreement.
- He or she never uses prayer manipulatively.
- He or she does not allow time to be wasted, but neither is in a rush.
- He or she does not pretend to consult, having already taken a decision.
- He or she allows laughter.
- He or she ensures everyone is given an opportunity to speak.
- He or she prepares properly for the meeting and has his or her papers in order.
- He or she ensures the agenda is adhered to, but does not stifle debate.
- He or she recognizes that his or her fellow PCC members are grown-ups.
- He or she does not talk too much and knows when to keep quiet.
- He or she gives a clear lead and is not afraid to support one view against another.

Helping to appoint a new minister

During a vacancy, sometimes termed an interregnum (that is, after one minister has left and before another has taken office), the churchwardens and the rural, or area, dean are in charge of the parish. Together with any other clergy or readers attached to the parish, they will need to provide for the pattern of worship and pastoral care to carry on as near normally as possible, to ensure that the PCC covers the costs of services, to take care of any vicarage or other property of the parish and to ensure that fees payable to the diocese (i.e. for weddings, funerals, etc.) are collected and accounted for in the usual way.

If the living is not suspended, a new incumbent will be chosen by the patron of the living, together with the bishop and two parish representatives appointed by the PCC. In some cases the bishop is himself the patron. If the living has been suspended, the patron is prevented from presenting and the bishop may proceed to appoint a priest-in-charge. This would normally be done in consultation with the patron and the parish. The bishop may have been waiting for an incumbent to move or retire before proceeding to pastoral reorganization, and it may take some time before a new arrangement is agreed between a number of parishes.

To assist in the appointments procedure, the PCC should prepare a parish profile, describing the nature and traditions of the parish and the characteristics desired in a minister. This could be begun with each member producing a description, and then everyone sharing what they have written. The profile can be expanded with details from the 2001 Census (the diocese might be able to provide these) and with a description of church life (other clergy, electoral roll, communicants, church groups, finances). Ideally this should have been prepared, or at least drafted, well in advance of the previous minister's leaving, as these are the kinds of decision best made when people are not feeling under a time-pressure or anxious about the future. Every minister will have to leave eventually (even if it is for the heavenly realms), so it can never be considered a waste of time to prepare a parish profile and person specification.

If presentation to the living is not suspended, the PCC also needs to appoint the two parish representatives, who should be lay people but need not be the churchwardens. If the PCC feels the ministerial position should be advertised, they should ask the patron to do so. The PCC can also suggest the name of an individual they would like the patron to appoint, but they cannot insist on their choice. The parish representatives can, however, veto a candidate put forward by the patron, as can the bishop, but they should be prepared to give their reasons for doing so. In practice, the patron, bishop and parish representatives will usually endeavour to come to a mutual agreement.

Working with the churchwardens

The office of churchwarden has three distinct aspects:

- the churchwardens of a parish are officers of the bishop;
- the churchwardens are the parish priest's principal collaborators;
- the churchwardens are the principal representatives of the laity on the PCC.

It is to be expected that the churchwardens will report to the PCC on any meetings they have had with diocesan officers and make clear to the PCC what their financial obligations are.

Specific duties of churchwardens

1. To keep proper records, including terrier of lands and inventory of articles belonging to the church.
2. To keep a logbook of alterations, additions and repairs.

3 To inspect the fabric and produce an annual fabric report.
4 To deliver the fabric report first to the PCC and then to the APCM, including an account of the inspection they have undertaken and of all actions taken or proposed for the protection and maintenance of the building and the implementation of the quinquennial inspection.
5 To provide answers to the Articles of Enquiry (a set of questions sent to each parish by the archdeacon) and complete the annual returns required by the diocese.
6 To present any matters they think ought to be brought to the bishop's attention.
7 To recruit, train and manage the sidesmen.
8 In conjunction with the sidesmen, to care for the safety, warmth and well-being of the congregation.
9 In conjunction with the sidesmen, to maintain order and decency in the church and the churchyard.
10 To be responsible for the cleanliness and overall appearance of the church and everything used, or worn, in it.
11 In conjunction with the sidesmen, to take, count, and lock away or hand over to the treasurer collections in church.
12 To attend meetings of the PCC and of the PCC standing committee as ex officio members.
13 To act as treasurer if the PCC fails to appoint another of its members to this office.
14 To ensure that the PCC meets its financial obligations.
15 To collaborate and co-operate with the incumbent in the carrying out of all the above duties, and in enabling the incumbent to carry out his or her own specific duties.
16 To have a duty of care towards the incumbent.

Working with the treasurer

It is important to remember that the treasurer is the PCC's treasurer, and that the PCC has collective responsibility for the finances of the parish, and members should therefore try not to get into the lazy habit of leaving everything to the treasurer, even if he or she is extremely competent. The treasurer needs the support of an informed PCC, whose members take the trouble to understand the accounts presented to them – both the year-end financial statements and the management accounts they receive throughout the year.

Management accounts

In order to make everyday financial decisions, the PCC needs something that looks very different from the annual accounts. The financial reports made to the PCC and its sub-committees are intended to provide a basis for arriving at decisions with financial implications, enabling members to answer the question: 'Can we afford to do this or that?' Church officers will also need information when involved in diocesan or deanery negotiation over the level of common fund or quota payment and when dealing with fabric matters, urgent repairs, etc. They need sufficient information to make a decision, and it should be provided in an easily understandable form.

Five columns of figures are helpful, and a sixth column – next year's budget – can be added towards the end of the financial year. (This is the first column in Figure 7.1.)

The second column gives the actual figure for last year (2006 in our example) to remind you of how things turned out.

Income	*Budget year 2008*	*Actual 2006*	*Budget year 2007*	*Profile %*	*Actual Jan–Nov 2007*	*Predicted out-turn*
Interest	8,000	8,293	9,000	80	7,193	8,000
Gift Aid	17,000	15,433	17,000	72	12,202	17,100
Plate	11,875	13,340	14,000	68	9,465	12,500
Box	18,050	18,385	19,000	96	18,326	19,000
Donations	10,000	13,593	14,000	125	17,532	18,000
Stewardship	45,000	33,083	37,000	89	32,764	38,000
Grants	0	8,743	0		0	0
Bookstall	13,400	14,219	16,000	73	11,722	14,200
Total	**123,325**	**125,089**	**126,000**		**109,204**	**126,800**

Expenditure	*Budget year 2008*	*Actual 2006*	*Budget year 2007*	*Profile %*	*Actual Jan–Nov 2007*	*Predicted out-turn*
Common Fund	43,372	50,003	47,000	92	43,083	47,000
Vicar's expenses	4,380	4,200	4,380	88	3,850	4,200
Staff costs	47,000	46,976	48,100	90	43,318	47,000
Church repairs	3,300	12,771	7,500	36	2,686	3,000
Utilities	7,000	7,648	8,000	72	5,741	6,500
Administration	11,000	11,385	12,000	85	10,219	12,000
Sundries	4,500	2,465	3,300	105	3,468	4,500
Total	**120,552**	**135,448**	**130,280**		**112,365**	**124,000**

Figure 7.1 Example of management accounts

The third column gives the budget for this year (2007 in our example); this was probably based on last year's budget using the historical method of budgeting.

The remaining three columns give the most recent figures. In our example they are for January to November – i.e. for eleven months of the year. The first figure here is the profile, showing what percentage of income or expenditure has taken place by now. The second is the actual figure to date, and the third is the predicted outcome (out-turn).

Profiling is the practice of predicting the pattern of expenditure across the financial year. It is a simple way to get a proper picture of income and expenditure. The budget year could be divided artificially into 12 equal portions of 8.3 per cent a month. On that basis 92 per cent of income should have been received and expenditure made by the end of November. This expectation could give an entirely erroneous view if Christmas collections, for example, are always very high and so December provides more than 8.3 per cent of income. In November, it might look as if you had a serious shortfall, but profiling – indicating that only 68 per cent of income from the collection plate has been received – shows that you expect to get more income. The actual figure to date really helps only when you have a profile and a realistic predicted out-turn. This final figure will become more useful and accurate in the last quarter of the year.

The financial year begins on 1 January and the PCC's budget should be agreed at the January PCC meeting at the latest. It should be possible to begin the budget process for the following year in September, on the basis of actual figures, profiling and predicted out-turn.

When treasurers talk about 'funds'

A *fund* may be defined as 'a pool of unexpended resources' – that is, a pot with money in it. Most of the money received by the PCC goes into a *general fund* that is *unrestricted*; that is to say, it can be used for any legitimate purpose. Money in an unrestricted fund might be *designated* – that is, intended at this time for use for a particular purpose, but not limited indefinitely to that purpose. The PCC may hold a number of designated funds earmarked for particular purposes, but those purposes can be changed.

'Do we have £600 to replace the choir cassocks?' the treasurer is asked.

Table 7.1 Restricted funds

Fund title	*Purpose*
Hymnbook fund	Begun in order to buy new hymnbooks five years ago, with the surplus to be used for subsequent repair and replacement
Chair fund	Begun three years ago to buy new chairs, with the surplus to be used for any future seating, and for repair and replacement
Peggy's flower fund	A legacy given to 'provide exotic blooms for Easter Day'
Bell fund	Moneys given for maintenance of the bells

'Well,' he says, 'we have £1,000 in the general fund, but we designated £200 of it to replace the big lawnmower and £400 for the boiler. If we don't need it for those purposes, the PCC can release it to the choir.'

There can also be *restricted* funds – that is to say, a pot with a label on it saying 'fabric' or 'organ' or whatever. Restricted funds have been given for a specific purpose and cannot be switched to any other purpose. The annual accounts may well show a number of restricted funds (see Table 7.1 above).

'Do we have £600 to replace the choir cassocks?' the treasurer is asked.

'No,' says he, 'for I am running a deficit on the general fund and all my other funds are restricted.'

'Let's start a choir cassock fund then,' says the vicar, 'and raise money specially for it.'

'A good idea,' replies the treasurer, 'but it would be better if you described it as a general cassock and vestment fund, or stipulated that any surplus would go into the unrestricted general fund of the PCC.'

Financial amateurs might think that a fund will actually have money in it available to spend, but the balance sheet will show where the money is (e.g. in a current account, in a Church of England Central Board of Finance (CBF) deposit account, on loan, etc.) and it may not be available immediately as cash. A wise treasurer will invest a restricted fund, especially if he or she realizes that it won't need to be liquid for several years. Incidentally, the interest on a restricted fund is also restricted to that purpose.

Working with committees

The standing committee

The PCC must have a standing committee of no fewer than five persons. The minister and churchwardens are ex officio members of the standing committee, which 'shall have power to transact the business of the council between meetings thereof subject to any directions given by the council'.[47]

The PCC is usually too large a body for the general discussion of ideas, but the standing committee can be the place where those who lead the parish can ask: 'What if we did so-and-so?' It can be a place for free thought, for exploring different, sometimes radically different, approaches, without formality, minutes or votes. It can be a place to fly a kite and not to worry if it won't fly. In order for this to happen, the standing committee members must trust each other and know that all members will keep the deliberations confidential. If someone violates that trust, the usefulness of the committee is undermined.

The standing committee, after working through its various ideas, needs to bring them to the PCC and not use its own powers to push them through. If it does this in a responsible way, it can become a 'think tank' for the parish, initiating and promoting positive and perhaps unexpected responses to challenges and opportunities.

Other committees

Although the standing committee is the only committee of the PCC that is required by the Church Representation Rules, parishes often find it useful to have a variety of committees, sub-committees and working groups – made up of PCC members and other members of the congregation – to carry out the detailed work of the PCC. In regard to such committees, the Church Representation Rules state: 'The council may appoint other committees for the purpose of the various branches of church work in the parish and may include therein persons who are not members of the council. The minister shall be a member of all committees ex-officio.'[48]

PCCs, however, sometimes go through cycles. Having set up a number of committees, the PCC itself becomes a body that reviews, monitors and approves the work of the committees. Members start to find the PCC meetings uninteresting, and feel that it has become

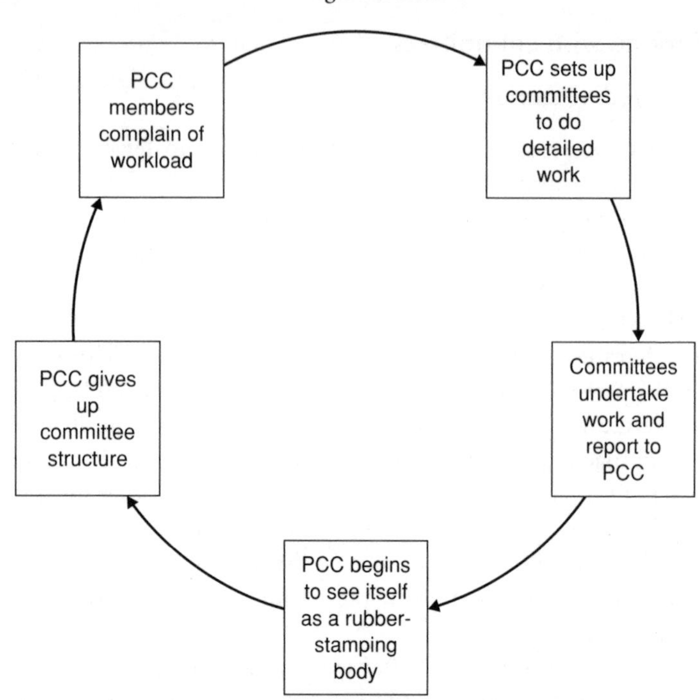

Figure 7.2 PCC committee growth and reduction cycle

a 'rubber-stamping' body. The number of committees is then reduced by the PCC, and more work is undertaken directly by the council. Meetings become longer and need to be more frequent. Members begin to complain that there is too much to do. Committees and working groups are set up, and the cycle begins again (see Figure 7.2). One purpose of the committees is that of ensuring that certain issues appear regularly on the PCC agenda, rather than of committees doing all the work on those issues.

Many sorts of committee may be found in a parish, according to need and to the mission priorities. This list is not exhaustive. Not every parish will require every sort of committee and some functions, such as fabric, buildings and property, might be combined in one committee.

Appointments committee

Although membership of the PCC is by open election, the council may have certain needs (for financial acumen, experience of property maintenance, knowledge of employment law, etc.) and can encourage suitably qualified people to stand for election. The committee can also identify suitable candidates for the offices of churchwarden, secretary, treasurer, etc.

Finance committee

This may exist as a PCC committee or as a sub-committee of the standing committee. It works with the treasurer and considers all aspects of church finance, including the preparation of the annual report and accounts.

Mission and ministry or pastoral committee

This committee ensures that the PCC gives time and attention to the mission of the Church and to the encouragement of ministry. Within its purview might be promotion of vocations, baptism preparation and follow-up, marriage preparation, bereavement support, ministry to the sick and housebound.

Youth and children's committee

This committee, working with the children's advocate (appointed by the PCC), ensures that the PCC considers matters affecting the young and children, including mother and baby/toddler groups, types of Sunday school and junior church, youth clubs and uniformed organizations.

Fabric committee

This committee oversees the implementation of the recommendations of the report made every five years by the designated inspecting architect (generally known as the quinquennial report).

Parish hall/parish centre or property and premises or buildings management committee

This committee looks after the parish hall (if there is one) and any other non-residential property. It ensures effective use and financial management, and deals with the policy on lettings (referring any long-term lettings to the diocesan authority), catering arrangements and building maintenance.

Fellowship or social committee

This committee initiates and organizes social events for the church and parish and uses the occasions to promote fellowship and to encourage the incorporation of newcomers into the church.

Education committee

This committee promotes the work of education in its broadest sense, but with a particular responsibility for the understanding of the Christian faith and for spiritual development.

Stewardship committee

This committee has the task of encouraging proper Christian stewardship of money and talents. It will be concerned to promote planned and committed tax-effective giving, as well as ensuring that the gifts and experience to be found in a congregation and parish are well used to promote the Church's mission.

Missions and charities or 'away-giving' committee

This committee encourages and promotes support for causes outside of the parish and makes recommendations to the PCC about the allocation of money made available for this purpose.

Ecumenical or Churches Together committee

The committee focuses on co-operation with and understanding of other Christian churches and promotes the Week of Prayer for Christian Unity.

Communications committee

This committee ensures that information is disseminated within the church and parish and the wider community. It may have responsibility for a parish website, e-mail newsletter, parish magazine, notice sheets, etc.

Worship committee

Some parishes find a need for a committee of this sort, though the ordering of worship is not the responsibility of the PCC. It may function as a working group, chaired by the minister, to co-ordinate the ministry of clergy, readers, servers, sidesmen and musicians.

Committees need to feed back into the PCC and frequently need PCC approval for policies or decisions. However, a PCC meeting which begins with a series of committee reports – finance, fabric, children, etc. – can be very tedious and, more significantly, can push deliberation on important matters to a time when people are tired and possibly irritable. PCCs do find it difficult to provide the sort of strategic direction that gives the green light to committees to pursue policies that are consonant with the strategy. One approach is termed 'green-amber-red'. Most matters are 'green' – areas in which an overall policy has been agreed, and in which committees and working groups can proceed subject to the policy and to any constraints on resources. Some matters are 'amber' and fall into boundary areas where there is good and sufficient reason for breaching a policy, perhaps after discussion with the minister and churchwardens. A few matters are 'red' and must be brought to the PCC for decision. The breakdown should be more or less: green 85 per cent, amber 10 per cent, and red 5 per cent.

We have found many examples of good practice in parishes, which has been shared by use of a parish website. St Stephen's, Canterbury,[49] for instance, drew up a parish plan which was simplified during 2004 as past plans had been 'enormous documents, with as many objectives as would be promoted by the United Nations!'. The parish plan, fairly straightforward in nature, made it clear to 'the whole body of the Parish, all the various congregations, volunteers, participants and well-wishers' what the parish wished to undertake and achieve during the ensuing year. The two-way responsibility of the committees to the PCC and the PCC's for the work of the committees was partially discharged through an annual review. Committees were asked to review what had gone well in the previous year, what had gone badly (or at least not as well as had been hoped), and what was planned for the next year. The mission committee reported as follows:

Two activities that went well:

✓Fair Trade Initiative (pancakes, stall, synod resolution) together with Trade Justice Initiative.

✓Fellowship Evenings, which have been on a broad range of issues and have provoked stimulating debate.

Two activities that did not go well:

✗Punch and Pudding Parties, where the uptake has recently been much less than expected, and which have not brought in more new people, despite all the work they entail.

✗The link with Madagascar, which has lacked purpose and personal interest.

Two activities that we should like to undertake next year:

★A Mission Sunday, involving Wayfinders and the Sunday school, perhaps with a visiting preacher, if possible developing trade and justice themes.

★Improving communication for fellowship and co-ordination with other Christians in Canterbury.

This approach has much to recommend it. First, it identifies things that were successful or fruitful during the year. PCCs often need encouragement, and this comes from recognizing what has gone well and building on it.

Second, it involves honesty about what hasn't gone well and why. It can seem brave at first to admit that an event which involved a lot of work, was carefully planned and well advertised, nevertheless failed. Many of the things that we try to do are unsuccessful or, at least, do not produce the anticipated result. Aware of limited resources, the PCC must sometimes say 'No' to a new initiative, or to the repetition of an old one which has not succeeded. New PCC members, making suggestions about things that might be done, don't want to hear older members say, 'We tried that in 1993 and it didn't work', but they might be helped by an account of why a similar venture didn't work on an earlier occasion. When it becomes normal to report honestly on what didn't work and why ('We couldn't do all we wanted to do because of lack of volunteers', 'We didn't allow enough time for proper organization of the patronal festival supper'), then these apparent failures can be used constructively. It can be particularly difficult if one of the things that didn't work was part of a diocesan initiative, such as a link with another country, province or diocese, but the diocese too needs to be aware of why an initiative failed.

Third, realistic targets for the coming year provide a degree of focus for people and resources. It is better to attempt something modest and do it well than to take on some great venture and fail completely.

Annual reporting should not, however, discourage projects that run over several years and belong to the core of the parish's vision or mission statement. A larger project can be broken up into manageable annual chunks.

Working with the wider congregation

The congregation needs to know who its PCC members are, and understand something of the issues that are dealt with and discussed at PCC meetings. A summary of PCC business will be provided in the annual report, and the main forum for members of the congregation to ask questions about the business of the PCC is the annual meeting. The Parochial Church Councils (Powers) Measure 1956 states that: 'In the exercise of its functions the parochial church council shall take into consideration any expression of opinion by any parochial church meeting.'

PCC members should of course be approachable at other times of the year and outside meetings, and be prepared to listen to the concerns of members of the congregation. It is important not to become allied with any disaffected groups or individuals, however, while remaining open to various points of view. Remember that the discontents within a congregation are also usually among the most vociferous; those who are perfectly contented with 'the way things are' are also probably far less likely to seek you out and tell you their opinion.

Like the churchwardens, you need to learn to establish a balance between representing the congregation on the one hand, and cooperating with the minister on the other. Ideally these two aspects of PCC membership should not be in competition. Occasionally they are, and then it is particularly important to avoid stirring up and exacerbating controversy. Try not to indulge in gossip and innuendo, and encourage others not to do so either. Make sure you are well informed about any issues under discussion and, when asked about them by members of the congregation, give accurate, unbiased information.

If you think there are things your minister needs to hear and to which he or she does not seem inclined to listen, then it is probably best to convey your concerns to the churchwardens for them to raise with the minister – but be specific, do not exaggerate, and avoid the construction, 'People are saying . . .'.

There is frequently a tendency in church circles to want to turn a mild controversy into a drama and a drama into a crisis. As a PCC member you have an opportunity to break this negative spiral and to help keep things in proportion. It is an opportunity which you should use.

♦ 8 ♦

Policies

Why various policy documents are necessary

The virtues of transparency and openness are now expected of all institutions, and the Church is no exception to this. It is, however, a new development in its history and calls for new approaches. In particular, various policies need to be enunciated, written down, agreed and made available for inspection – policies that in previous eras might merely have been 'understood', without the perceived need for formal agreement.

As the people responsible for the mission of the Church of England in a parish or benefice, usually including the stewardship of a building or buildings and of money given to promote the work of the Church, the churchwardens and other PCC members carry significant responsibility. Properly worked-out policies on various issues represent an important aspect of the fulfilling of that responsibility – and can also save time as once a policy has been decided, there should be no need to go on endlessly discussing it (apart from reviewing it, probably on an annual basis).

Collective ownership

It is important that policies agreed by the PCC are collectively owned by the council and that once a decision has been made, it is supported by all the members, particularly when talking to other members of the congregation.

Examples of various policies

Statement of insurances

The PCC is responsible for ensuring that there are adequate insurances in place, but members are often unaware of the policies, the valuation and the cost of insurances. The churchwardens should ensure that a report is made to the PCC each year (see Dudley and Rounding, *Churchwardens: A Survival Guide*, pp. 77–9).

Child protection and young people

A PCC policy on child protection and young people, though tailored to the needs of the local parish, must be based on the recommendations of the Church of England House of Bishops' Policy on Child Protection and any guidelines issued by the diocese (each diocese may have its own variations), as well as meeting the requirements stated under the Children Act 1989 and the Home Office's guidelines. Your diocese may well provide a model statement which it advises parishes to adopt without additions or changes. The policy should be reviewed annually. The PCC must also ensure that it has adequate insurance cover, including public liability insurance, for all activities organized by the church and held at the church that involve children.

Fire precautions and risk management

Free-standing churches without offices or staff working on the premises used not to be covered by any fire or safety legislation, but are now subject to the Regulatory Reform (Fire Safety) Order 2005, which came into effect on 1 April 2006. In addition, churches that are also workplaces are covered by legislation concerning health and safety and are subject to inspection by the local fire brigade.

The PCC should undertake a fire-risk assessment and keep it available for inspection by the fire authority. This entails a structured and systematic examination of the workplace to:

- identify hazards from fire;
- decide if a hazard is significant;
- decide who is at risk;
- decide whether the existing fire precautions are inadequate;
- make an action plan to minimize the hazard.

A written emergency plan must then be prepared to indicate the action that people should take in the event of a fire. Together the fire-risk assessment and emergency plan should:

- identify all the significant risk hazards;
- identify who is at risk from each fire hazard;
- evaluate existing control measures to see whether they reduce risk to a tolerable level;

- determine what additional measures are required;
- describe the means of escape from the premises in case of fire;
- describe the means of detection and of giving warning in case of fire;
- describe the means of fighting the fire;
- include planning for an emergency;
- provide for training, information and instruction to staff about fire precautions in the workplace (if applicable);
- provide for effective maintenance and testing of fire-safety equipment and precautions.

An assessment will almost certainly identify some areas of concern. (For an example of a PCC fire policy see Dudley and Rounding, *Churchwardens: A Survival Guide*, pp. 82–3.)

> St Paul's fire protection policy? *Above all, taking the shield of faith, wherewith ye shall be able to quench all the fiery darts of the wicked.* [Ephesians 6.16]

[Just be grateful we haven't included St Paul's equal opportunities policy.]

Disability access and audit

The Disability Discrimination Act 1995 states that it is unlawful for a provider of services to discriminate against a disabled person in refusing to provide, or in deliberately failing to provide, the disabled person with any service that he or she provides, or is prepared to provide, to members of the public. The expression 'provision of services' includes the provision of any goods or facilities and access to and use of any place that members of the public are permitted to enter. Churches, therefore, fall under the provisions of the Act and it would be unlawful to discriminate, whether deliberately or by an act of omission, against any disabled person, whether in regard to worship or in access to a building. The Act goes further in stating:

> Where a provider of services has a practice, policy or procedure which makes it impossible or unreasonably difficult for disabled persons to make use of a service which he provides, or is prepared to provide, to other members of the public, it is his duty to take such steps as it is reasonable, in all the circumstances of the case, for him to have to take

> in order to change that practice, policy or procedure so that it no longer has that effect.
>
> Where a physical feature (for example, one arising from the design or construction of a building or the approach or access to premises) makes it impossible or unreasonably difficult for disabled persons to make use of such a service, it is the duty of the provider of that service to take such steps as it is reasonable, in all the circumstances of the case, for him to have to take in order to –
>
> (a) remove the feature;
> (b) alter it so that it no longer has that effect;
> (c) provide a reasonable means of avoiding the feature; or
> (d) provide a reasonable alternative method of making the service in question available to disabled persons.

A PCC has a duty to inspect the building or buildings used for its various purposes and to appraise accessibility, judging against predetermined standards (e.g. of space needed for wheelchair access). The PCC will certainly focus on the church building and the extent to which steps or other obstacles limit access, but must also be aware that a disabled person could be prevented from joining in activities (such as Bible study, PCC meetings, etc.) that took place in a private house that was not accessible for such a person.

Alteration to a building, especially a historic building, to remove the obstacle created by a physical feature creates all sorts of difficulties and adds a further burden of cost, but the PCC is required to carry out an access appraisal and to take all reasonable steps to provide access.

A PCC should:

1 Discuss disability access and appoint an 'access officer' to be responsible for ensuring that the matters raised are dealt with. The officer should talk to disabled people and their carers, and to members of the congregation and visitors who use wheelchairs and pushchairs, or have difficulty with hearing or with steps, etc.
2 Look for simple solutions: changing the way you do something is simpler than changing the building.
3 Consult the inspecting architect or surveyor about possible structural alterations.
4 Draw up an action plan, with a timetable and a budget.
5 Consult the archdeacon.
6 Seek the advice of the DAC and others, in the normal way, before proceeding to a faculty application.

Complaints policy and procedure

All churches receive complaints from time to time. These may be directed to the bishop, archdeacon or rural (or area) dean, or directly to the incumbent or the churchwardens. While not encouraging complaint, we should remain open to genuine dissatisfaction and all complaints should be treated seriously and investigated fully and fairly. Most complaints can be dealt with informally but a formal procedure can aid resolution. A good system is that of appointing someone who is generally respected, but is not a member of the PCC, to be a complaints officer. If that person has some legal training or related experience, so much the better. With these principles in mind (and probably including them in a preamble to a complaints policy), a PCC might adopt a policy like that in the following example:

Example: Policy on complaints

We will always try to deal with complaints addressed to the minister, churchwardens or other officers informally and in an amicable fashion where possible. Complaints addressed to the bishop, archdeacon or area dean are generally referred back to the minister but must be dealt with in whatever way the bishop directs.

Our complaints procedure is divided into informal and formal stages. We would expect that the majority of complaints can be dealt with informally.

Complaints will be dealt with on as confidential a basis as possible, but the person who first receives a complaint will need to discuss it with those who can resolve it, so anonymity and total confidentiality cannot be expected.

The procedures set out below are for complaints made by persons entered on the church electoral roll, members of the congregation, visitors and others who participate in the life of the church or receive its ministry. Other procedures will be set up to deal with specific types of complaint, e.g. by a member of staff.

A copy of this document will be given to any person who initiates a complaint.

Informal stage If anyone (other than a paid employee of the church) wishes to make a complaint, it should normally be addressed to the minister. If it is a complaint concerning the minister, it should be addressed to the churchwardens. Many concerns arise from misunderstandings and can be resolved by simple clarification. If the minister or churchwardens consider a complaint too serious for the informal stage, then they will immediately commence the formal stage. If the complainant is not satisfied with the way in which a complaint is dealt with during the informal stage, then he or she may request that the formal stage be initiated. The churchwardens and other officers are required to bring all complaints to the attention of the minister.

Formal stage The formal procedure begins with logging the complaint in a confidential logbook, which will contain the date of the complaint, a brief outline of it, a summary of the steps taken to resolve it and the outcome.

The complaint will then be passed to a 'complaints officer' (a designated person who is not a member of the PCC). The complaints officer or a person or persons nominated by him or her (who shall not be members of the PCC) will investigate the complaint. The complaints officer will, as necessary, seek the advice of the diocesan registrar.

A confidential file will be kept on each individual formal complaint while it is investigated.

The complaints officer will advise the complainant if a complaint that alleges breach of the ecclesiastical law should be addressed to another person or body.

The complaints officer will determine what steps should be undertaken to resolve the complaint.

Members of staff and officers of the church against whom a complaint is made will be kept fully informed of the investigation being made and will be given a written statement at the end of the investigation.

The person making the complaint will be informed in writing of the outcome of the investigation and the action taken.

Any complainant who is not satisfied with the way in which a complaint is dealt with is at liberty to renew the complaint to the diocesan bishop. The complaints officer shall then send to the bishop a copy of the confidential file and an account of his or her investigation of the complaint.

♦ 9 ♦

Troubleshooting

In this section we want to look at what happens when the PCC follows all the proper procedures and it still goes wrong.

A little monograph of five pages published in Cambridge in 1930 and written by someone with the initials B.R.F.G. was entitled *The Failure of the Parochial Church Councils.* It looked at the objects for which PCCs had been founded, pointed to the main object, the primary duty of the council 'to co-operate with the incumbent in the initiation, conduct and development of Church work both within the parish and outside', and declared the councils to be failures because:

> They confine their efforts to the raising and expenditure of money. They are far more interested in the Fabric than in the spiritual welfare of the Church. In many-too-many cases, as those whose work brings them into intimate personal touch with the parochial clergy know full well, they are so far from co-operating with the incumbent as to be a sharp thorn in his side.

Why is this? B.R.F.G. thought that those who had created the relevant Measures had no knowledge either of human nature or of public affairs:

> It should have been obvious, for instance, that in many parishes the Councillors would sooner or later be acutely and, perhaps, equally divided upon some point of administration or policy. In every such case the incumbent must needs have an opinion of his own on the one side or on the other; and the result is that if one party applaud his wisdom, the other for ever sets the smallest value upon his intelligence.

He also thought that the people most suited for membership of the council would not accept nomination and that it would be filled with 'those whose chief characteristics are pushfulness and a fine disregard of the feelings and susceptibilities of other people', who are ready seekers 'after a little brief authority' and he had a deep concern that: 'The sensitive heart of the Church is in the Central Fund, the heart of the Diocese is found at the Board of Finance, and . . . the Parochial Church Council is nothing but a business body, and not a missionary body even in intention'.[50]

Much of what B.R.F.G. had to say still rings uncomfortably true today.

Sources of conflict

The peace of the church community can be broken by conflict emanating from a number of sources. One such powerful source is the General Synod. Certain policies adopted by the Synod have a clear effect on parish life and notable recent examples have been liturgical change, the ordination of women and the Anglican–Methodist Covenant. When a PCC is invited to discuss a contentious matter, it will often divide into majority and minority viewpoints. Where the matter is distant or theoretical, division may be of little consequence, but when it concerns life in the parish – 'Shall we accept an ordained woman here or not?' – then the result may be serious conflict and division.

Another area of concern is conflict with the local community. The most frequent trigger points are planning matters, the use of the church building, graveyard questions, pastoral reorganization and the possibility of closing the church.

The largest generator of conflict, however, is internal – clashes between people and groups within the church community that purport to be concerned with policies and theologies but are usually much more about people, their likes, their dislikes, and their sometimes bitter enmities.

Conflicts of interest

PCC members do sometimes have conflicts of interest. The Charity Commission defines a conflict of interest as 'any situation in which a trustee's personal interests, or interests which they owe to another body, and those of the charity arise simultaneously or appear to clash'. A broader view is that a conflict of interest is a conflict between the official responsibilities of a person in a position of trust and any other interests the particular individual may have, where the individual could be seen to be influencing church matters for actual or potential personal benefit or to benefit some other body, group or individual. An interest can be simply 'personal' or it can be 'personal and prejudicial'.

The PCC does not keep a register of members' interests, so it is necessary to declare at a meeting if one has an interest. A member would have a *personal* interest if discussion at PCC concerned, for instance, the Scout group of which their son was a leader, or the letting of the church hall to the Scottish dance club to which they belonged, or the giving of a donation to St John Ambulance in which they served as a volunteer. A member would have a *personal and prejudicial* interest, and should state it before withdrawing from the meeting, if the discussion concerned the redevelopment of land adjoining their property, or the award of the auditing contract to their accountancy firm, or even the payment of choir wedding fees when they sang in the choir. If in doubt, a member should seek the chairman's advice or else declare a possible interest and let the chairman rule on it.

One particular aspect covered in the Charity Commission's publication on the general responsibilities of charity trustees (CC3), available from the Commission, is of relevance to the PCC, and that is the answer to the question: 'Can trustees be paid for their duties?' The answer given is as follows: 'Generally, no. Trustees are not entitled to receive any payment out of the charity's property other than reasonable and necessary out-of-pocket expenses. Furthermore they cannot directly or indirectly benefit personally from the charity.'[51]

So can someone who is employed by the PCC – such as an administrator, organist, gardener, builder, etc. – be a member of the PCC? The answer would appear to be 'No', even though there is nothing about it in the Church Representation Rules, except with reference to the PCC secretary and treasurer who, if they receive remuneration, cannot be members of the PCC. The need for the proceedings of the PCC to be utterly transparent would seem to rule out the membership of anyone employed by the council in any capacity, because it cannot be clear that, having a financial interest, they can act impartially on any matter that has financial implications.

What about the clergy? Some clergy feel uncomfortable with chairing the PCC because they are paid by the Church of England. The clergy, however, are office-holders rather than employees (though this may change), and the stipend is not set by the parish or parishes they serve. This effectively removes any conflict of interest. Nevertheless, there will be business at PCC meetings in which the minister has a personal interest (e.g. the level of clergy expenses), and for these items he or she must declare an interest and, as necessary, hand the chair to the vice-chairman, refrain from voting or even leave the meeting for the duration of the discussion.

There are other sorts of vested interest. Let us suppose that a member of the PCC was also a trustee of another charity that used the church building or the church hall. In general there might be no conflict of interest, but there may be occasions (setting the rent, for instance, or deciding which organizations should be allowed to use the hall) when the member must declare an interest. It will be for the chairman to determine whether the person can be heard on the matter, while not being permitted to be party to the discussion or have a vote on the matter. The rules that apply elsewhere must be observed in church matters too.

Removing the pews: an example of conflict resolution

The worship sub-committee of the PCC explored, at the invitation of the minister, alternative approaches to worship, in order to ensure that all constituencies in the parish were provided for. The review was very thorough and undertaken with full consultation. The recommendations included changing the timing and nature of a number of Sunday services, and the sub-committee also reached the conclusion that the removal of some of the Victorian pews – one or two at the front of the church, four on each side at the back, near the font – would facilitate greater movement and dignity in worship. The proposal from the worship sub-committee was passed to the fabric committee, discussed in the standing committee and, after consultation with the inspecting architect, the archdeacon and the DAC, it came before the PCC. The various difficulties were ironed out, and the resolution authorizing the vicar and churchwardens to apply for a faculty was carried *nem. con. Nem. con.* here meant that one member of PCC had abstained from voting, but had not asked that her abstention be recorded. No one voted against and no member of the PCC was absent from the meeting. The plans were submitted to the DAC and sent to English Heritage, the Council for the Care of Churches and two amenity societies for comment. They were put up on a display board at the back of the church and attention was drawn to them in the parish magazine. The DAC agreed the proposal and the documents were returned, duly stamped. The public notice, inviting objections, was displayed on the external and internal notice-boards early in September.

At the October PCC meeting, the vicar read out a letter from a former member of the congregation objecting to the removal of the pews, and another letter, from an occasional worshipper, supporting it. The diocesan registrar had received a number of letters, mostly objecting to the change. Most of the objectors seemed to be using the proposal as a peg on which to hang complaints about other things. One of the churchwardens presented a draft letter of response to the objectors setting out quite clearly the reasons for the intended course of action.

At the February meeting, the vicar reported the receipt of a letter from a Campaign Objecting to the Removal of Pews (CORP), copied to the bishop, the archdeacon, the patrons of the living, and the Archbishop of Canterbury! This claimed that the churchwardens' letter to objectors was intimidatory. The group claimed to represent 109 objectors, who were not named, and it blamed the 'leaders of the parish' for fomenting unrest and creating division. It was alleged that the PCC was not wholly in favour of the decisions, that members were afraid of the vicar and churchwardens, and that they had been coerced into voting in favour. Dissenters, it claimed, had been excluded from the PCC by vote-rigging at the APCM and the vicar was only appointing 'yes-men' to office in the church. A number of members of the PCC were angry at the suggestion that they were unable to make up their own minds and to express their views at PCC meetings. The vicar wrote to CORP explaining the situation in which the decision had been reached, and pointing out that neither the secretary nor the other objectors who had written actually worshipped at the church.

The diocesan registrar visited the church and met with the vicar and with the secretary of CORP. It emerged that the real argument was about changes in worship and not about removing pews. The registrar hoped it might be possible to achieve a compromise and, without further discussion, extended the period of notice for the lodging of formal objections. In due course the application came before the diocesan chancellor and, with certain conditions, was granted. All members of the PCC shortly received a letter from CORP accusing the vicar of bullying and harassment, of destroying the church's Prayer Book tradition and, for good measure, mentioning suspected financial irregularities and marital infidelity. The letter was copied to archbishop, bishop, archdeacon, patron and rural dean, to which were now added the local MP and the district council. The next day the vicar received a call from the local newspaper. The journalist had a list of the vicar's sins of omission and commission – removing artificial flowers from the churchyard, refusing to agree a design for a gravestone with a photograph of the deceased, sacking the organist, refusing to silence the church clock at night, financial mismanagement, and so on. The report in the local newspaper – someone pinned it to the parish notice-board – was followed by tabloid interest and might have ended with the vicar, beleaguered and depressed, resigning, except for one thing: the churchwardens and PCC gave the vicar total support.

Vicar and PCC followed all the proper procedures, consulted widely, and gave opponents a chance to have their say. It should all have been decided by the grant of a faculty but the opponents of change shifted their tactics, widening the scope and content of their allegations and objections. It was the vicar, as figurehead and chairman, who took the brunt of the attack. It was intended to undermine the vicar in the sight of the church authorities, and to separate the vicar from the PCC. While the initial objective was that of reversing the decision about the pews, it soon developed into a campaign to get rid of the vicar. It was because such campaigns, in which the clergy become targets, have become more frequent that we wrote our earlier book, *The Parish Survival Guide*. The proposal to remove pews triggered what we called there the 'dust ball' phenomenon – of little consequence in itself, it became a focus, rolling along and gathering up complaints of various sorts, many of them from those who had left the church some time ago. Once a focus has been found, the opponents initiate a campaign of destabilization, generating a sense of unease and anxiety in the parish.

If members of the PCC voted for the proposal because they believed it was right, then they had a responsibility to accept the consequences of that decision. In doing so, they could rely on the fact that they, not the objectors, were regular worshippers, knew the needs of the congregation, and had been elected to office. PCC members can be a stabilizing force, putting out the flames rather than fanning them, reassuring people and affirming that the proposal and the vicar had, and continue to have, the full support of the members of the PCC.

When we cannot agree: anger in the PCC

The first of the two scenarios with which we began this book – the angry vicar coming home, the angry PCC members in the pub, the angry resignation from membership – was, we hope, not typical, but many, perhaps most, clergy, churchwardens and PCC members will have experienced angry meetings in which pent-up frustration has erupted. Although there has been a growth in the business of anger management, few writers consider anger and the way it can build up in the Church.[52] One psychology textbook deals with anger only as a reaction to stress, part of the frustration–aggression hypothesis that assumes that whenever a person's effort to reach a goal is blocked, an aggressive drive is induced that motivates behaviour to injure the object or person causing frustration. Direct aggression is not always possible, because the source of frustration is too vague and intangible, or too powerful, but the anger is there and seeks an object and outlet. This can give rise to displaced anger, directed at an innocent person or object rather than toward the actual cause of frustration.[53]

Anger is listed among the seven deadly sins. The sense that anger is a bad thing creates difficulties in managing it, so people repress it or try, ultimately ineffectively, to control it, or else they blow up. Anger, as one handbook on clergy stress says, prevents us from carrying out our best insights, jaundices our perspective (particularly towards certain people and issues) and, even when controlled, can communicate itself to others as simmering below the surface.[54] In the work environment, we are exposed to all sorts of annoyances and irritations, and these give rise to anger, if they are not dealt with, or else they exacerbate existing anger.

The first person to be described as angry in Scripture is Cain, who was very angry about Abel, and slew him. We can read of the anger of Jacob, of Pharaoh, of Moses, of Saul and of David, and so on but, as Robert Thurman says in his little book on anger (see note 52), in the Jewish Bible the angriest person around seems to be God. Thurman, professor of Indo-Tibetan Buddhist Studies at Columbia University, describes God as getting mad in the Garden of Eden, cursing the serpent, Eve, Adam and the ground. He is angry with Cain, angry with human beings prior to the Flood, angry at the tower of Babel, nice to Abraham, but gets mad about Sodom and Gomorrah, and gets really mad with Pharaoh. In sum, says Thurman,

> he gets angry with people again and again. He gets angry on behalf of Israel and sometimes he gets angry at Israel. He's a real punisher. Anyone who was indoctrinated by sacred texts in the image of such a God as the model of ultimate reality personified could be forgiven if he or she thought that anger was an excellent energy and manifestation, as long as one was powerful enough to overcome the enmity such anger stirs up in others.

Certainly the Book of Common Prayer expresses a rather similar view of God. We are miserable sinners and God is entitled to be angry with us. The confession at Morning and Evening Prayer asks God to have mercy on us, and asks him too to spare – that is, to refrain from punishing – those who confess their faults. The Litany asks the Lord to 'remember not our offences' and to spare us, pleading 'spare thy people, whom thou hast redeemed with thy most precious blood, and be not angry with us for ever'. If you want a really strong example of this conviction that the wrath of God will consume sinners, then look towards the back of the Prayer Book, at the Commination 'or denouncing of God's anger and judgements against sinners'. And the cry constantly goes up: spare us, have mercy on us, enter not into judgement with us, turn thine anger from us. The Prayer Book comes into existence at the end of the Middle Ages, a period in which much hope and optimism departed from the Western Church. Some historians think that the Black Death of the 1340s, which dramatically reduced the population of Europe, cast a long shadow over Christian spirituality. It was seen as judgement, and the wrath of God had to be appeased. As the Church set out to do so, by penitential acts, by processions, litanies, psalm-saying and by offering masses, so the Reformers responded by stressing faith and grace and the Scriptures. The Reformation was supposed to remove any doubts that believers had about justification and salvation, but the Church of England preached the risk of impending destruction, of the outpouring of the wrath of God. We might consider the extent to which this stress on a factor characteristic of the Old but not the New Testament was culturally conditioned, the product of experience, and we might wonder if it was a means of social control, of instilling morality, utilized by the unscrupulous Tudor state – yet we are left with a question that is theologically, spiritually and personally significant, the question of the wrath of God.

Our first experience of anger is probably an angry parent. Children are inclined to push to the limits, doing what they have been specifically forbidden to do. What follows used to be, maybe still is, parental anger: 'You will make me very cross if you do that, if you go on doing that.' It could be parental disappointment, an approach adopted in the 1970s by those who did not do anger: 'I am very disappointed in you for doing what I asked you not to do.' Reasonableness replaces anger, though it might be a form of repressed anger. And if a child constantly pushes to the limit and beyond – what does the parent do then? Rage? Or seek counselling? Or turn to drink? Anger, when not irrational or displaced, is related to limits and the crossing of boundaries, to rules and their violation. Now when the law, in the person of a judge, deals with deliberate law-breaking, he or she may point to the cold-blooded calculated disregard for the law and for norms of civilized behaviour, and society's anger is expressed in punishment and in the level and duration of this punishment. Anger is there, but it is in a way sublimated.

If God has, directly or indirectly, brought us into being, and is concerned – passionately concerned – about our well-being, and has provided us with direction and purpose and with certain rules and limitations, and we have ignored these, pushed to the limit and beyond, broken rules deliberately and without thought of the consequences, and put our lives and the lives of others and the future of all of us at risk, then one possible response for God the Creator, alongside disappointment and deep concern and maybe even a feeling of disempowerment, is anger and a desire to punish those who will not take telling.

This is not an analysis we will like very much. It puts us in the position of naughty human child faced by angry parent God. If we allow this view to dominate our faith, to shape our spirituality, to affect the way in which we relate to those in authority in the Church, then it generates a form of infantilism. When this child–parent approach dominates parish life then there is also a tendency to direct our complaints and problems upwards, to a higher parental authority, especially the bishop, rather than to deal with difficulties in a mature and responsible way.

When we talk of divine wrath we must always remember that we are talking about God, of whom the prophet says: 'My ways are not your ways, says the Lord.' In other words, God is different from us, and the language that we use is analogical, taking what we know about and applying it to what we know much less about. So we are struggling to describe our relationship, and one part of it is that we are a disappointment to God, who expects so much more of us because he has given us the gifts, the abilities, the powers that enable us to be god-like and we have perverted them and made, more than once, hell on earth. More in sadness than in anger, God might behold the creation.

The language of wrath used to describe God, and the pleading tone we adopt as we ask for pardon, may be figurative, but the reality is that we fall short of the target and this failure is, to some extent at least, our fault. The failure covers personal and social relations, questions of the environment and the future and, because this is our concern here, love of neighbour and our relationships with the Church. The psalmist suggests in a number of places that we address the relationship that this all-embracing failure creates, and further suggests that we might be sorry. And seeing that we are wrong and admitting we are, and realizing that such a failure at such a level has consequences, he suggests that we might ask to be spared the consequences, while seeking the grace to amend our ways. There should be no disjunction between our prayers, private and corporate, and our service of the parish on the PCC. We acknowledge, for example, in the Prayer Book Collect for the first Sunday after the Epiphany that we need divine aid 'to perceive and know what things [we] ought to do' together with 'the grace and power faithfully to fulfil the same'. We know too that 'all our doings without charity are nothing worth' and that we need 'that most excellent gift of charity, the very bond of peace and of all virtues'[55] in order to achieve what is really of value in the life of the Church and parish. Anger does not promote the 'bond of peace', so how can we deal with it?

The spiritual writer Henri Nouwen found that he had to deal with anger during the seven months in which he was part of the Trappist community at the Abbey of the Genesee in upstate New York. Speaking with his mentor Fr John Eudes, Nouwen identified the features of anger:

> I realized that my anger created restlessness, brooding, inner disputes, and made prayer nearly impossible. But the most disturbing anger was the anger at myself for not responding properly, for not knowing how to express my disagreement, for external obedience while remaining rebellious from within, and for letting small and seemingly insignificant events have so much power over my emotional life. In summary: passive aggressive behaviour.[56]

Together Nouwen and Fr John Eudes produced five suggestions for dealing with this anger:

1 Allow your angry feelings to come to your awareness, and have a careful look at them. Don't deny or suppress them, but let them teach you.
2 Do not hesitate to talk about them, even when they seem to be related to very small or seemingly insignificant issues. If you can't deal with anger over small things, how will you deal with a real crisis?
3 There can sometimes be good reason for anger. Talk about it. Find out whether it is unrealistic or disproportionate. Find out why you have responded so strongly.

4 Part of the problem might be generalization: a disagreement about a decision, an idea, an event, might make you angry with someone, or with everyone.
5 Anger often reveals how you think and feel about yourself and how important you have made your own ideas and insight. If you re-centre on God, then you get a better idea of your own importance, or unimportance.

Anger reappears in Nouwen's diary for the next month or so but then gradually disappears as he enters more into the life of the community and bothers less about his status as a 'celebrity spiritual writer'. We can all use these suggestions but the difficulty is finding someone – a critical friend – with whom to share these feelings, someone who can be trusted and who can also provide some insight. William E. Hulme identifies two therapeutic approaches to anger: cathartic (let it out) and cognitive (change the way you think) – and an approach that combines them, involving identification of cause and appropriate expression of anger.[57]

There is plenty on the Web about anger and anger management, and the American Psychological Association site is particularly useful for its definitions and the strategies for keeping anger at bay, namely:

- relaxation;
- cognitive restructuring (changing the way you think);
- problem-solving (acknowledging that not all anger is misplaced);
- better communication (listen to what is underlying the anger);
- using humour;
- changing your environment.[58]

Redford Williams, an internist and behavioural specialist at Duke University Medical Centre, has developed a 12-step programme that can help people learn to deal with their angry emotions:

1 Monitor your cynical thoughts by maintaining a 'hostility log'. This will teach you about the frequency and kinds of situation that provoke you.
2 Acknowledge any problems in coping with anger.
3 Seek the support of important people in your life in coping with your feelings and in changing your behaviour patterns.
4 By keeping your hostility log you are able to realize when and where you are having aggressive thoughts, so that when you find yourself in these situations you can utilize such techniques as

deep breathing, positive self-talk, or thought-stopping, which can help you interrupt the anger cycle.

5 Put yourself in the other person's shoes. This will help you gain a different perspective. Keep in mind that we are all human beings, subject to making mistakes.
6 Learn how to laugh at yourself and see humour in situations.
7 Learn how to relax. Although you may have heard that expressing anger is better than keeping it in, remember that frequent outbursts of anger are often counterproductive and may alienate others.
8 It is also important that you practise trusting other people. It's usually easier to be angry than to trust, so by learning how to trust others you are less likely to direct your anger at them.
9 Good listening skills improve communication and can facilitate trusting feelings between people. This trust can help you deal with potentially hostile emotions, reducing and possibly eliminating them.
10 Learn how to assert yourself. This is a constructive alternative to aggression. When you find yourself angry at another person, try to explain to them what is bothering you about their behaviour and why. It takes more words and work to be assertive than it does to let your anger show, but the rewards are worth it.
11 If you live each day as if it were your last, you will realize that life is too short to get angry over everything.
12 The final step requires forgiving those who have angered you. By letting go of resentment and relinquishing the goal of retribution, you will find the weight of anger lifted from your shoulders.[59]

We suggest that a PCC agenda should allow for time at the end of a meeting to look at what went well, what went badly, and why. This is particularly important if there have been angry outbursts and people have been hurt by what has been said or done. We must always remember that this is a Christian body, a council made up of Christians; we may disagree with each other, but we should attempt to limit the damage caused by such disagreements. This is another of the responsibilities that rests on all members and not just on the clergy.

> *Let all bitterness, and wrath, and anger, and clamour, and evil speaking, be put away from you, with all malice: And be ye kind one to another, tenderhearted, forgiving one another, even as God for Christ's sake hath forgiven you.* [Ephesians 4.31–2]

When people feel they have to make a complaint

It does happen, unfortunately, that minister and people sometimes fall out and cannot achieve reconciliation. A parish is, as we have stressed, a local expression of Christ's Church, a community that should have love as its characteristic sign. There are mechanisms for dealing with disagreements, and it is only right to use the Clergy Discipline Measure 2003 if all other methods have been tried and have failed.

Under the Measure, disciplinary proceedings may be instituted against an archbishop, bishop, priest or deacon, alleging any of the following acts or omissions:

a) doing any act in contravention of the laws ecclesiastical;
b) failing to do any act required by the laws ecclesiastical;
c) neglect or inefficiency in the performance of the duties of his office;
d) conduct unbecoming or inappropriate to the office and work of a clerk in Holy Orders.[60]

Proceedings are initiated by laying a complaint; in the case of a priest or deacon, this may be done by:

i) a person nominated by the parochial church council of any parish which has a proper interest in making the complaint, if not less than two-thirds of the lay members of the council are present at a duly convened meeting of the council and not less than two-thirds of the lay members present and voting pass a resolution to the effect that the proceedings be instituted; or
ii) a churchwarden of any such parish; or
iii) any other person who has a proper interest in making the complaint.[61]

The complaint is to be made to the bishop and must be accompanied by written particulars of the alleged misconduct. Written evidence in support of the complaint must also be sent to the bishop either with the complaint or at such later time as he may allow.

Once a complaint is laid there is a procedure to be followed, which begins with scrutiny of the complaint by the diocesan registrar in order to determine if it is a valid complaint. If it is, the bishop has a number of courses of action open to him – namely, to take no further action (though this can be challenged by appeal); to put the matter on record conditionally and without penalty; to seek conciliation between the parties; to impose a penalty by consent (where the offence is admitted); or to move towards formal investigation and a hearing.

It will be seen that the use of the Clergy Discipline Measure is a serious matter with possible consequences both for the complainants and for the respondent. The focus of this book is the PCC, and it must be noted that the PCC can nominate a person to make a complaint against one of the parish clergy only at a properly constituted meeting, convened in accordance with the Church Representation Rules. The minister (who may be the subject of the complaint) is still entitled to be present and to chair the meeting!

The complaint must state:

- the bishop to whom the complaint is made;
- the full name and contact address, including postcode, of the complainant;
- the name and position held of the priest or deacon about whom the complaint is made;
- why the complainant claims to have a proper interest or is otherwise entitled to make the complaint and, if the complainant is nominated by the PCC, a certified copy of the resolution must be attached;
- in summary form, the nature and details of the acts or omissions alleged to be misconduct;
- the date or dates of the alleged misconduct (which must not normally be more than a year ago);
- the evidence in support that the complainant relies upon, which shall be in writing, signed and dated by the maker of the statement in each case.

There must be a declaration that the complainant believes the facts of the complaint to be true, and the complaint must be signed and dated by the complainant and be sent or delivered to the bishop.[62]

The Measure does allow for one particular form of reckoning. A minister may leave a parish and it is only after he or she has gone to another parish or even another diocese that the PCC discovers irregularities caused, perhaps, by inefficiency or neglect of duty. The PCC is entitled to lay a complaint within a year against its former minister to the bishop of whichever diocese the minister has moved to, and may feel that it ought to do so in order to avoid a repetition of the behaviour.

The full text of the Measure can be purchased from OPSI or be downloaded from <http://www.opsi.gov.uk/measures/20030003.htm>.

♦ 10 ♦

End of period in office

Whether to stand for re-election

When you come to the end of your term of office, you will need to decide whether to stand for re-election (unless your APCM has agreed a maximum term and you have reached it). Things affecting your decision will include your knowledge of the time commitment involved as well as your awareness of whether there are a number of other members of the congregation desirous of their 'turn' on PCC. A degree of continuity is important and the ideal PCC will contain a mixture of experienced and newer members, so if you feel you definitely still have something to contribute and would like to stand for re-election, there is no reason why you should not do so. But remember that there are plenty of other opportunities for serving your church community even without being on PCC. Your PCC membership, and the insights you have gained, will certainly not have been wasted.

Whether to become a churchwarden

Someone who already has experience of being on PCC, who has enjoyed that experience and feels ready to embrace further challenges in the service of the church community, may make an ideal candidate for the position of churchwarden.

A churchwarden needs to be someone who commands the respect of the minister, the PCC and the congregation, can be available for consultation, is willing to make decisions in collaboration with others and to carry them through, is ready to listen, is a skilled communicator and can facilitate communication between others.

To be effective, a churchwarden needs to devote quite a lot of time to the job, becoming conversant with the main areas of responsibility as well as being prepared to get to know the congregation that has elected him or her to office. Time must be a factor in reaching this decision; if you cannot afford to give the time, do not stand for the office.

You will need to be a regular attender at church so that you become a familiar face. A churchwarden does not need to go to everything all of the time, but he or she does represent the eight o'clock and Evensong congregations as well as the Parish Eucharist congregation, the Tuesday morning Communion group as well as the Thursday Bible class. A churchwarden needs to know what is going on and who the regular members of each congregation are. You also cannot be a churchwarden if you expect to be away every year at Christmas or Easter!

Anyone who is qualified and can find a nominator and seconder can stand for election; no one has to wait to be asked. It would still be sensible, however, to declare an interest in being churchwarden early on and to discuss it with the incumbent and with the existing wardens. A churchwarden-in-waiting, and willing to wait, can be very useful, especially when illness, sudden death, the demands of a job or some other matter unexpectedly leads to vacation of office.

Qualifications for becoming a churchwarden

In order to be eligible for election to the office of churchwarden you must fulfil all of the following criteria:

1. Your name must appear on the church electoral roll of the parish where you are going to stand.
2. You must be an actual communicant.
3. You must be 21 years of age or older.
4. You must not be disqualified under various pieces of legislation.
5. You must not have already served as churchwarden of the same parish for six successive periods of office since the passing of the Churchwardens Measure 2001 (No. 1).

A person is disqualified from standing for election to the office of churchwarden if he or she:

- is disqualified from being a charity trustee under Section 72(1) of the Charities Act 1993 (c.10);
- has been convicted of any offence mentioned in Schedule 1 to the Children and Young Persons Act 1933 (c.12);
- is disqualified under Section 10(6) of the Incumbents (Vacation of Benefices) Measure 1977 (No. 1).

♦ 11 ♦

Serving the parish

In conclusion, here are some thoughts for servants of the parish to consider:

- The Church's foundation is Jesus Christ her Lord. Church notice-boards tend to declare 'Church of England, Diocese of such-and-such' when the fundamental message ought to be that each and every parish is part of the 'Apostolic Church of Jesus Christ'. The first purpose of the parish, rooted and grounded in Christ, is to proclaim the good news.
- As incarnational, the Church is both a divine and a human institution. The local church is an expression of the universal Church. The Church is both divine in its institution, as shown by its titles 'Bride of Christ' and 'Body of Christ', and human in its structures and ministry. Vicars, churchwardens and PCCs are not divinely instituted per se, and only have value in so far as they serve the purposes of the Church's mission.
- The parish does not need to be strictly territorial or geographical. Parishes will have a geographical core, a place for ministry, but the parish can also have an impact on various networks to which people belong. Being grounded in a place enables rather than hinders the mission of the parish.
- The parish needs to be visibly part of the episcopal church. The Church of England is episcopally ordered; every parish is within a diocese and under the care of the bishop. Various circumstances have made the relationship between parish and bishop difficult in recent years, but the diocesan bishop remains the chief pastor of the diocese. The authority of ministry is conveyed through the bishop, and a parish neither should be nor is free to separate itself from the bishop's ministry.
- The parish needs to be missionary in orientation, geared towards and expecting church growth. One of the questions sometimes asked of charities is: 'If you were founded today, would you be doing what you are doing?' For parishes, the answer is often in

the negative. A beautiful historic parish church or a decaying Victorian red-brick building can be equal burdens on a parish, which can become a society for preserving a historic building. This is clearly not what the local church is meant to be. The building cannot be ignored, and it may be – and very often is – an asset, but focus on the building can work against mission. The PCC needs to put the building into context, and the context is created by the whole mission of the Church.

- The parish is a Christ-centred eucharistic community. Central to the parish is a core community – it may be just the biblical two or three, or it may be very large – centred on Christ and sharing, through the Eucharist, in communion and fellowship, with Christ and with each other. This core community, working constantly to draw more people towards it, sustained by prayer and by mutual love, in accordance with Christ's command, has the duty of ensuring that the parish remains focused on worship and mission.
- We need to be more imaginative about ways to be the Church in a given place. The obsession with buildings, their repair and maintenance, has stifled our imaginations. We end up being imaginative only about ways to raise money for the fabric fund. Neither should we be anxious when other parishes seem more successful than our own in various aspects of their ministry; instead we should be prepared to learn from them. Each parish flourishes when all parishes flourish.
- We should not assume that we have any more right to be heard than any of the other voices which claim people's attention today. In consequence, we have to present the Christian message in an effective way, aware that some will think of it as hopelessly old-fashioned, as organized superstition or as completely alien. We certainly need imagination, but we don't need gimmicks. We need fidelity to the gospel and faith in the work of the Holy Spirit in our parish, in the communities and networks that we serve.

Appendices

Appendix 1

Parochial Church Councils (Powers) Measure 1956

1 Definitions

In this Measure –
'Council' means a parochial church council;
'Diocesan Authority' means the Diocesan Board of Finance or any existing or future body appointed by the Diocesan Synod to act as trustees of diocesan trust property;
'Minister' and 'Parish' have the meanings respectively assigned to them in the Rules for the Representation of the Laity.

2 General functions of council

(1) It shall be the duty of the minister and the parochial church council to consult together on matters of general concern and importance to the parish.

(2) The functions of parochial church councils shall include –
  (a) co-operation with the minister in promoting in the parish the whole mission of the Church, pastoral, evangelistic, social and ecumenical;
  (b) the consideration and discussion of matters concerning the Church of England or any other matters of religious or public interest, but not the declaration of the doctrine of the Church on any question;
  (c) making known and putting into effect any provision made by the diocesan synod or the deanery synod, but without prejudice to the powers of the council on any particular matter;
  (d) giving advice to the diocesan synod and the deanery synod on any matter referred to the council;
  (e) raising such matters as the council consider appropriate with the diocesan synod or deanery synod.

(3) In the exercise of its functions the parochial church council shall take into consideration any expression of opinion by any parochial church meeting.

3 Council to be a body corporate

Every council shall be a body corporate by the name of the parochial church council of the parish for which it is appointed and shall have perpetual succession. Any act of the council may be signified by an instrument executed pursuant to a resolution of the council and under the hands or if an instrument under seal is required under the hands and seals of the chairman presiding and two other members of the council present at the meeting at which such resolution is passed . . .

7 Miscellaneous powers of council

The council of every parish shall have the following powers in addition to any powers conferred by the Constitution or otherwise by this Measure –

(i) Power to frame an annual budget of moneys required for the maintenance of the work of the Church in the parish and otherwise and to take such steps as they think necessary for the raising, collecting and allocating of such moneys;

(ii) Power to make levy and collect a voluntary church rate for any purpose connected with the affairs of the church including the administrative expenses of the council and the costs of any legal proceedings;

(iii) Power jointly with the minister to appoint and dismiss the parish clerk and sexton or any persons performing or assisting to perform the duties of parish clerk or sexton and to determine their salaries and the conditions of the tenure of their offices or of their employment but subject to the rights of any persons holding the said offices at the appointed day;

(iv) Power jointly with the minister to determine the objects to which all moneys to be given or collected in church shall be allocated;

(v) Power to make representations to the bishop with regard to any matter accepting the welfare of the church in the parish.

Appendix 2

Charities Act 1993

Persons disqualified from being trustees of a charity

72. (1) Subject to the following provisions of this section, a person shall be disqualified for being a charity trustee or trustee for a charity if –

(a) he has been convicted of any offence involving dishonesty or deception;

(b) he has been adjudged bankrupt or sequestration of his estate has been awarded and (in either case) he has not been discharged;

(c) he has made a composition or arrangement with, or granted a trust deed for, his creditors and has not been discharged in respect of it;

(d) he has been removed from the office of charity trustee or trustee for a charity by an order made –

(i) by the Commissioners under section 18(2)(i) above, or

(ii) by the Commissioners under section 20(1A)(i) of the Charities Act 1960 (power to act for protection of charities) or under section 20(1)(i) of that Act (as in force before the commencement of section 8 of the Charities Act 1992), or

(iii) by the High Court,

on the grounds of any misconduct or mismanagement in the administration of the charity for which he was responsible or to which he was privy, or which by his conduct contributed to or facilitated;

(e) he has been removed, under section 7 of the Law Reform (Miscellaneous Provisions) (Scotland) Act 1990 (powers of Court of Session to deal with management of charities), from being concerned in the management or control of any body;

(f) he is subject to a disqualification order under the Company Directors Disqualification Act 1986 or to an order made under section 429(2)(b) of the Insolvency Act 1986 (failure to pay under county court administration order).

(2) In subsection (1) above –

(a) paragraph (a) applies whether the conviction occurred before or after the commencement of that subsection, but does not apply in relation to any conviction which is a spent conviction for the purposes of the Rehabilitation of Offenders Act 1974;

(b) paragraph (b) applies whether the adjudication of bankruptcy or the sequestration occurred before or after the commencement of that subsection;

(c) paragraph (c) applies whether the composition or arrangement was made, or the trust deed was granted, before or after the commencement of that subsection; and

(d) paragraphs (d) to (f) apply in relation to orders made and removals effected before or after the commencement of that subsection.

(3) Where (apart from this subsection) a person is disqualified under subsection (1)(b) above for being a charity trustee or trustee for any charity which is a company, he shall not be so disqualified

if leave has been granted under section 11 of the Company Directors Disqualification Act 1986 (undischarged bankrupts) for him to act as director of the charity; and similarly a person shall not be disqualified under subsection (1)(f) above for being a charity trustee or trustee for such a charity if –

(a) in the case of a person subject to a disqualification order, leave under the order has been granted for him to act as director of the charity, or

(b) in the case of a person subject to an order under section 429(2)(b) of the Insolvency Act 1986, leave has been granted by the court which made the order for him to so act.

(4) The Commissioners may, on the application of any person disqualified under subsection (1) above, waive his disqualification either generally or in relation to a particular charity or a particular class of charities; but no such waiver may be granted in relation to any charity which is a company if –

(a) the person concerned is for the time being prohibited, by virtue of –

(ii) a disqualification order under the Company Directors Disqualification Act 1986, or

(ii) section 11(1) or 12(2) of that Act (undischarged bankrupts; failure to pay under county court administration order), from acting as director of the charity; and

(b) leave has not been granted for him to act as director of any other company.

(5) Any waiver under subsection (4) above shall be notified in writing to the person concerned.

(6) For the purposes of this section the Commissioners shall keep, in such manner as they think fit, a register of all persons who have been removed from office as mentioned in subsection (1)(d) above either –

(a) by an order of the Commissioners made before or after the commencement of subsection (1) above, or

(b) by an order of the High Court made after the commencement of section 45(1) of the Charities Act 1992;

and, where any person is so removed from office by an order of the High Court, the court shall notify the Commissioners of his removal.

(7) The entries in the register kept under subsection (6) above shall be available for public inspection in legible form at all reasonable times.

Further reading

Atrill, P. and McLaney, E., *Management Accounting for Non-Specialists*, Pearson Education, Harlow, 3rd edition, 2002.

The Canons of the Church of England: you can buy a copy or download them from <http://www.cofe.anglican.org/about/churchlawlegis/canons>.

The Charities Act 1993 and the PCC, 2nd edition 2001, published for the Finance Division of the Archbishops' Council by Church House Publishing: available from Church House Publishing and can also be downloaded from <http://www.cofe.anglican.org/info/papers/charact/index.html>.

Church Representation Rules, Church House Publishing, London, 2006.

Derkse, W., *The Rule of Benedict for Beginners: Spirituality for Daily Life*, Liturgical Press, Collegeville, MN, 2003.

Dudley, M. and Rounding, V., *Churchwardens: A Survival Guide*, SPCK, London, 2003.

Dudley, M. and Rounding, V., *The Parish Survival Guide*, SPCK, London, 2004.

House of Bishops, *Protecting All God's Children: The Child Protection Policy for the Church of England*, Church House Publishing, London, 2004.

Hudson, M., *Managing Without Profit*, Directory of Social Change, London, 1999.

Hulme, W.E., *Managing Stress in Ministry*, Harper & Row, San Francisco, CA, 1985.

The Layman in Church Government – Being a Guide to The Representation of the Laity Measure, 1956 and The Parochial Church Councils (Powers) Measure 1956, The Church Information Board, London, 1956.

Mission-Shaped Church: Church Planting and Fresh Expressions of Church in a Changing Context, Church House Publishing, London, 2004.

Oswald, R.M. and Koroeger, O., *Personality Types and Religious Leadership*, Alan Institute, Washington DC, 1988.

Ranken, W.B., *Good Employment Guide for the Voluntary Sector*, 4th edition, NCVO, London, 2005.

Useful websites

<http://www.blackburn.anglican.org/yellow_pages/index.htm> contains a directory of church-related services and businesses.

<http://www.careofchurches.org.uk/> – the Council for the Care of Churches.

<http://www/charity-commission.gov.uk> is the website of the Charity Commission.

<http://www.chpublishing.co.uk/index2.asp> – Church House Publishing, the official publisher of the Church of England.

<http://www.cofe.anglican.org/> – the Church of England's own website.

<http://www.dsc.org.uk/> – the website of the Directory of Social Change, which provides information and training for the voluntary sector.

<http://www.ecclawsoc.org.uk/cases/index.shtml> has summaries of many of the legal cases reported in the *Journal of the Ecclesiastical Law Society*.

<http://www.ecclesiastical.co.uk> is the website of the Ecclesiastical Insurance Group.

<http://www.english-heritage.org.uk/server/show/nav.1122> – the part of English Heritage's site which gives details of the Repair Grants for Places of Worship Scheme.

<http://www.historicchurches.org.uk/> – the Historic Churches Preservation Trust.

<http://www.hmrc.gov.uk/charities/claim_tax_back.htm> is the part of HM Revenue and Customs' site where you can find details of how the Gift Aid scheme works.

<http://www.john-truscott.co.uk> – the website of the church consultant and trainer, John Truscott, contains some very useful ideas for everyone involved in church management. Some of his 'Training Notes' are particularly interesting and helpful.

<http://www.ncvo-vol.org.uk/askncvo/hr/> – for all matters on employment and working with volunteers.

<http://www.opsi.gov.uk/> – the website of the Office of Public Sector Information which provides online access to UK legislation.

Diocesan websites

Diocesan websites vary enormously in terms of content and usefulness to parishes (and some do their best to hide their most useful pages). Here is a selection of the better sites, with specific links to resources for parishes, where available:

Bath and Wells:
<http://www.bathandwells.org.uk/changing_lives/parish_resources/index_pr.php>
Birmingham:
<http://www.birmingham.anglican.org/article/26/>
Blackburn:
<http://www.blackburn.anglican.org/> (consult the A–Z listing at this site)
Bristol:
<http://www.bristol.anglican.org/> (click on Downloadable Resources)
Canterbury:
<http://www.canterbury.anglican.org/parish/index.htm>
Carlisle:
<http://www.carlislediocese.org.uk/support/>

Chester:
<http://www.chester.anglican.org/ministry/ParishSupport/>
Chichester:
<http://www.diochi.org.uk/> (click on Resources)
Ely:
<http://www.ely.anglican.org/information/>
Exeter:
<http://www.exeter.anglican.org/css/css-downloads-parishadmin.php>
Gloucester:
<http://glosdioc.org.uk/downloads/downloads.htm>
Guildford:
<http://www.cofeguildford.org.uk/html/resources.shtml>
Leicester:
<http://www.leicester.anglican.org/resources/index.html>
London:
<http://www.london.anglican.org/Regulations/>
Newcastle:
<http://www.newcastle.anglican.org/info/parish_resources_pcc.htm>
Oxford:
<http://www.oxford.anglican.org/parishresources/>
St Albans:
<http://www.stalbans.anglican.org/resources/resources.html>
St Edmundsbury and Ipswich:
<http://www.stedmundsbury.anglican.org/#> (follow the links under Administration)
Sheffield:
<http://sheffield.anglican.org/index.php> (follow the links under What We Do)
Southwark:
<http://www.southwark.anglican.org/resource/index.htm>
Southwell and Nottingham:
<http://www.southwell.anglican.org/resources.html>
Wakefield:
<http://www.wakefield.anglican.org/support/issues/index.htm>
York:
<http://www.salvonet.com/diocese_of_york/adminandinfo6.shtml>

Notes

1. <http://www.cofe.anglican.org/info/socialpublic/>.
2. *Mission-Shaped Church: Church Planting and Fresh Expressions of Church in a Changing Context*, London, Church House Publishing, 2004, p. xi.
3. *Mission-Shaped Church*, p. 8.
4. *Mission-Shaped Church*, p. 18.
5. Mike Hudson, *Managing Without Profit*, London, Directory of Social Change, 2nd edition, 1999.
6. Dean Inge, 'The Problem of Authority', in *Church of England Newspaper*, 1 November 1929.
7. House of Lords: Judgement – Parochial Church Council of the Parish of Aston Cantlow and Wilmcote with Billesley, Warwickshire (Appellants) v Wallbank and another (Respondents), 2003.
8. See Wil Derkse, 'Listening and Responding: Benedictine Spirituality in Non-Monastic Contexts', in *Logos: A Journal of Catholic Thought & Culture*, Vol. 3:3, University of St Thomas, Saint Paul, MN, 2000 <www.stthomas.edu/cathstudies/logos/derkse.html>.
9. Hymn 260 in *The English Hymnal*, Oxford, Oxford University Press, 1933 edition.
10. Roy M. Oswald and Otto Koroeger, *Personality Types and Religious Leadership*, Washington DC, Alan Institute, 1988.
11. See <www.cditrainers.org>.
12. <http://www.cditrainers.org/Ben%20spirit%20-%20cong%20dev.htm>.
13. From an address given at the Trinity Institute's 34th National Conference, 'Shaping Holy Lives: Benedictine Spirituality in the Contemporary World', 2003.
14. <http://www.charity-commission.gov.uk/supportingcharities/ogs/Glossary.asp>.
15. <http://www.charity-commission.gov.uk/supportingcharities/ogs/Glossary.asp>.
16. We should point out that in our earlier book *The Parish Survival Guide* we made the mistake of saying that PCCs were 'exempt' charities. PCCs are not exempt from Charity Commission (CC) supervision but they are, currently, excepted from having to register with the Commission.
17. Letter from the Charity Commission to one of the authors, 3 September 2004.
18. Peter Atrill and Eddie McLaney, *Management Accounting for Non-specialists*, Harlow, Pearson Education, 3rd edition, 2002, p. 136.
19. *The Layman in Church Government – Being a Guide to The Representation of the Laity Measure, 1956 and The Parochial Church Councils*

(Powers) Measure 1956, London, The Church Information Board, 1956, p. 21.

20 *The Charities Act 1993 and the PCC*, 1.4.
21 CC61 – *Charity Accounts: The Framework*, p. 3.
22 For more details about what might go into an annual report, see Martin Dudley and Virginia Rounding, *Churchwardens: A Survival Guide*, London, SPCK, 2003, pp. 70–6.
23 SORP 2005, paras 244–5.
24 *The Charities Act 1993 and the PCC*, 1.27.
25 <http://www.charity-commission.gov.uk/investigations/charrisk.asp#4>.
26 CC61, p. 8.
27 Albert Mitchell, *The Enabling Act and the Powers Measure*, London, Church Book Room Press, 1947, p. 85.
28 Contained in: House of Bishops: *Protecting All God's Children: The Child Protection Policy for the Church of England*, London, Church House Publishing, 2004.
29 Mitchell, *Enabling Act*, p. 94.
30 Church Representation Rules: 12(3).
31 CRRs: 18(1).
32 <http://www.lichfield.anglican.org/lichfield/rugeley/hednesford/information.html>.
33 From the brief guide to the Synodical Government (Amendment) Measure 2003.
34 CRRs: General Provisions relating to Parochial Church Councils 1(c).
35 CRRs: General Provisions relating to Parochial Church Councils 1(f).
36 CRRs: 1(8).
37 CRRs: 11(9).
38 CRRs: 2(1).
39 CRRs: 2(1).
40 CRRs: 2(6).
41 CRRs: 2(7).
42 CRRs: General Provisions relating to Parochial Church Councils 4(c).
43 CRRs: General Provisions relating to Parochial Church Councils 3.
44 CRRs: General Provisions relating to Parochial Church Councils 4(b).
45 CRRs: General Provisions relating to Parochial Church Councils 4(b).
46 CRRs: 15.
47 CRRs: General Provisions relating to Parochial Church Councils 14(b).
48 CRRs: General Provisions relating to Parochial Church Councils 15.
49 See <http://www.ststephenscanterbury.net/>.
50 B.R.F.G., *The Failure of the Parochial Church Councils*, Cambridge, W. Heffer & Sons, 1930.
51 CC3: *The Essential Trustee: What You Need to Know*, p. 13.
52 It is discussed by Robert Thurman, from a predominantly Buddhist point of view, in the New York Public Library series on the seven deadly sins, published by Oxford University Press in 2005 and simply entitled *Anger*.

53 Rita L. Atkinson et al., *Introduction to Psychology*, 10th edition, 1990, pp. 562–3.
54 William E. Hulme, *Managing Stress in Ministry*, San Francisco, CA, Harper & Row, 1985, p. 84.
55 Prayer Book Collect for Quinquagesima.
56 Henri Nouwen, *The Genesee Diary*, Garden City, NY, Doubleday, 1981, p. 44.
57 Hulme, *Managing Stress*, pp. 86–91.
58 <http://www.apa.org/topics/controlanger.html>.
59 <http://www.angermanagementseminar.com/articles/management_coping_with_anger.html>.
60 Clergy Discipline Measure 2003, Section 8(1).
61 Clergy Discipline Measure 2003, Section 10(1)(a).
62 The Clergy Discipline Rules 2005, Section 4(2).

Index